WOUNDED
SOLDIER

JOHN STEER

New Leaf Press

First printing: December 1997

ISBN: 0-89221-375-2
Library of Congress Number: 97-75889

Cover by Janell Robertson

DEDICATION

I want to dedicate this book to all those who care —
care about their God, care about their country, and especially to those who care about their fellow man.

To Cliff Dudley — without Cliff there would be no
book. He and his lovely wife and children continue to be
an inspiration and encouragement to me. Tim (who I see
very rarely) and I have a special bond. Thanks for your
help and friendship, Tim.

I want to thank Mom and Dad, who put up with a very
rebellious son. But they had faith that somehow I would
make it. Thanks to Lynn and Leigh Hampton who have
been a true source of help, inspiration, and friendship for
many years.

I want to dedicate this book to those three million
plus who served in Vietnam, and millions more who
served their country stateside or in other countries.

Last but not least, I dedicate this book to my wife and
partner, Donna, and our four beautiful children, Monique,
John, Sarah, and David, who have sacrificed much over
the years to follow me around the world and support my
ministry.

CONTENTS

PREFACE

As you read my testimony and get an idea of where I've been and some of the things I've done, I hope that you will begin to understand the mercy our Lord had for me — and *has* for you.

I did not write this book because I am proud of my old life. Neither did I write it to become famous or to make a fast buck. I wrote this book because the Holy Spirit dealt with my heart.

It was very painful for me to go back over all the details of my life and expose myself before you. But the Lord put me together with Cliff Dudley, and without his help this book would never have been written.

As we spent many long hours re-living and writing about my past, Cliff gave me love and encouragement.

You may have similar problems to those I had. Your life may be filled with booze or drugs. Or maybe you just hide your feelings and pretend everything is all right.

If it is all right, why do you feel guilty?

Why do you hate yourself?

Why aren't you happy with your wife and kids?

Why do you sometimes get knots of hate in the pit of your stomach?

Why do you say in your heart, "Nobody understands, nobody cares"?

Maybe you think I'm a sissy because I had so many problems and had to turn to Jesus for help.

You may claim to have it all together. I hope you do. But many Vietnam vets are committing suicide, turning to drugs and alcohol, and getting killed in car wrecks.

In fact, John P. Wilson, Ph.D., who conducted the "Forgotten Warrior" research project for the DAV (Disabled American Veterans), believes the suicide rate among Vietnam veterans is much higher than the national average. Some stats say as many as 200,000 Vietnam vets have committed suicide or died a violent death such as driving into a bridge while intoxicated.

In addition, many Vietnam veterans also have marriage problems. Of those veterans who were married before going to Vietnam, 38 percent were divorced within six months after returning from Southeast Asia.

Between 40 and 60 percent of the veterans of the Vietnam War have persistent problems with emotional adjustment. The number of Vietnam veterans hospitalized for alcoholism or drinking problems has more than doubled in the past seven years.

Today, the problems are getting worse, not better. To you who have problems — and to you who think you don't have any problems — I have the answer: Give your heart and life to Jesus Christ.

Some may say, "I've tried religion." I'm not talking about religion. I'm talking about a personal experience with Jesus Christ, the author and finisher of our faith.

When I went through jump school at Fort Benning, Georgia, it took every fiber of my being to get through it. The same was probably true of the training you took. If you would put half that much effort into seeking the Lord, He will meet you.

Jesus said, "Ask, and it shall be given you; seek, and you shall find; and to him that knocks it shall be opened" (Matt. 7:7).

Remember also that "all things work together for

good to them that love God and are called according to his purpose" (Rom. 8:28).

If God loves me why did He allow me to go to Vietnam and to see and do all the terrible things I did and saw? Because He knew that is what it would take to break me and cause me to repent and serve Him.

"For whom he did foreknow, he also did predestinate to be conformed to the image of his Son" (Rom. 8:29).

Jesus knew I would eventually serve Him. I praise Him for not letting me die out there and go to hell, and for not taking His hand of protection off me. I'm beginning to understand how much God loves me.

Vietnam — was it a curse or a blessing? A little of both.

≈ ❚ ≈

My rebelliousness reminds me a little of an experience I had with my oldest son John. I was rolling out some barbed wire to put up a fence. John, who was nine, asked, "Can I roll it out, Daddy?"

"No," I said, "you will get scratched up."

Although he had no gloves on, John continued to persist: "No, I won't. No I won't."

"Yes, you will," I said.

Finally, I realized he needed a lesson; otherwise he would never believe me. I let him roll out the wire, and he got his hands all scratched up. Now, maybe the next time I tell him something he will believe me.

I didn't allow him to get scratched up because I don't love him — I did it because I *do* love him. He persisted in having his own way.

And so it is with the Lord. He has a perfect plan for your life. But until you decide to do it His way, you are going to get scratched up.

Listen for that still small voice beckoning you to accept Him and serve Him. Jesus is the ONLY answer.

For speaking or concert information, or to receive a catalog on John's books, tapes, or musical CD's, please write:

John Steer
2851 Thornhill Road
Winter Haven, FL 33880

Cassette tapes:
"When I See Old Glory"
"It's a Little Country"
"Preacher Man"
"Requested Favorites"
"Peace in the Valley"
"Cowboy's Journey"
"Country Gospel"
"Circuit Rider"
"Wounded Soldier" (newest tape)

CD's:
"When I See Old Glory"

Books:
Faces I Tried to Forget

CHAPTER 1

No Turning Back

G et in line."
I obeyed immediately, knowing this would be the first of many commands.

The young men standing rigidly in front of me must have been thinking the same thing. No one talked or moved.

Nervously holding my enlistment papers, I said to myself, *Man, I hope this is the right thing to do.* Then I remembered: I had no choice. This was my only way out.

"John, I don't want to see you end up in prison," my dad had said. "Maybe if you join the army, things will be better for you."

For the first time in our lives Dad and I had come to the same conclusion. "Yeah, maybe it will help me turn my life around," I agreed.

So far I had screwed up everything. As a high school dropout, I had been to 11 schools just to get through the ninth grade — and the last was reform school. Growing up in the inner city of Minneapolis, I had learned early to steal, smoke, and drink. Dopers, pimps, prostitutes, alcoholics — you name it — these were our neighbors.

As an angry and violent teenager, I was fast with a knife and quick to fight my way out of any confrontation. It didn't take me long to realize that the law of the "city jungle" meant survival of the fittest. The toughest and the strongest wins;

the weakest gets beat up! I read every martial arts book I could get my hands on and taught myself how to break boards with my fists.

Many of the neighborhood guys had been involved in rape, incest, immorality, stealing, booze, and drugs.

The girls were always on the take — trying to get us boys to go to bed with them. The attention made me feel proud because I was looking for security, friendship, and someone to love. I was a candidate for anything.

Ironically, the charge that sent me to jail was for something I hadn't done. My girlfriend accused me of rape. Although she later told the truth, I was still put on probation and charged with "carnal knowledge."

"What about my record?" I had asked my dad.

"Right now with the war in Vietnam, the army needs soldiers," he had said. "We can probably get a judge to give you a waiver."

I'll never forget the day Dad and I went to the court-house in St. Paul together. It was one of the few times I felt he had supported me. In fact, as a boy, I had been terrified of my dad.

One day in particular stood out in my mind. When I entered the third grade, the teacher soon discovered I couldn't read and wanted to put me back a grade.

When he found out, Dad went into a rage. He sat me down, put a book in front of me, and said, "Read this!"

I couldn't read it.

He hit me and screamed, "Now, read this!"

Again, I couldn't read it.

He hit me again, and screamed at me: "Now, read this!"

I couldn't. I was shaking violently, and the more I shook, the more he hit me and screamed. I didn't think it was ever going to end.

As I stood before the judge in the St. Paul courthouse, pleading my case, the words were determined, "I want to straighten up and make something of myself."

The judge must have believed me because he com-pletely cleared my record. "If you want to join the army," he told me, "you shouldn't have any trouble getting accepted."

Dad and I looked at one another and smiled.

I was on my way.

⇌

"You're next!" The army recruiter shouted at me as he looked up from the papers stacked in front of him. "Name!"

"John Steer."

As he wrote, I asked, "What's 'airborne'?" I had heard the guy ahead of me mention he wanted "airborne."

"You get paid $55 more a month," the sergeant answered, "and you jump out of airplanes."

I had thought only guys with an education could be paratroopers. "Okay," I said. "Sign me up for it — airborne."

"You got it!" the recruiter replied smugly.

"I want electronic maintenance engineering," I reminded him. My main goal was to receive some kind of training I could use later in life. "Since I'm volunteering, I can get that, right?"

"Right," the sergeant said with a sarcastic smile.

As soon as I signed up, the recruiters started laughing and joking.

"What's so funny?" I asked.

"I want to tell you something, boys," he replied. "There's only two things that come out of the sky — idiots and bird crap. Which are you?"

I knew then that I'd done something wrong! Within a short time, I discovered that being "airborne" waived any additional training. Although the disappointment at not becoming an electronics specialist nearly broke my heart, I was determined not to give up.

I told myself: *I've never succeeded at anything in my life, but this time I'm going to do the very best I can.*

⇌

"If I have my way, you will go to jail and never get out!" Although I was almost dead drunk, those words quickly sobered me up.

In the week since I had signed up for the army, I had gone wild — like an animal who knows he's going to be caged.

I had learned to smoke and drink at an early age. In fact, my dad taught me.

One day when I was about 12 years old, I was in the laundromat with Mother and decided to confide in her. She seemed to be treating me like an adult so I said, "Mom, I'm going to tell you something: I'm smoking."

"Oh, I know that, John. I've been finding tobacco in your shirts, and I could smell it on you," she replied.

"Mom, all my friends smoke in front of their parents" (that was a lie), "and I think I should be able to smoke in front of you — can I?"

"No, no. We'll have to talk to your Dad about it."

"Oh, Mom, please don't tell Dad," I begged.

You guessed it — she told him.

"John," Dad called, "smoking, huh?"

"Yes, sir," I remarked trying to act big.

"Well, as long as you're smoking you might as well smoke a man's smoke."

He gave me a cigar and lit it. I smoked one cigar, then another. Dad was getting upset with me because I was puffing and inhaling those cigars like a man. Then he said, "Boy, as long as you're smoking you might as well drink, too."

"Boy this is great, Dad," I said feeling high and mighty. That was all I'd ever seen my dad do — smoke and drink. I thought that was the way to become a man.

He got the booze and started pouring us shot glasses of whiskey. He'd drink one, and I would drink one. I was really feeling good. I didn't realize that he was determined to make me sick; I thought he was trying to be my buddy. Then I started to get sick, but I had such a strong will I wouldn't let him know.

When he got up to go to the bathroom I ran into my bedroom, found an old bathrobe and vomited in it, wiped off my face, and went back in the living room and sat down.

When he came back from the bathroom, Dad never knew that I had left — the cigar was still glowing in my hand.

He looked at me rather startled and said, "Okay, John, that's enough for now, but we're going to do this every night when I come home from work."

The next day at school I told everybody, "Man, my dad lets me smoke and drink. I'm going to do it with him tonight when I get home. Don't you wish you had a dad like mine?"

I got home from school and eagerly waited for him. Finally, when he came home I said, "Dad, I'm ready."

When he found out what I was talking about, he knocked me from one end of the house to the other. He was furious! I don't know which hurt more — the beating or the disappointment of realizing Dad had only been putting me on. I didn't quit smoking or even slow down; however, I never did it around my parents again.

Now, the day before I had to report for duty, the police had pulled me over for speeding and running stop signs. The skid marks on the road gave them an open and shut case.

The girls I had with me in the car were not helping the situation. They offered the policemen beer and invited them to come in the car and join the party.

"We're going to take you in," the patrolmen taunted. "If you have an ace in the hole, you'd better play it now, kid."

"I've got one." Reaching up above the visor, I pulled out my enlistment papers that stated I was going into the service the very next day.

"Man, that's the only ace that could keep you out of jail," the cop said, "You better get out of here and not cause any more trouble."

The next day I boarded the train for Fort Leonard Wood. The tough ladies' man from the night before had suddenly been replaced by a scared teenager leaving home heading for uncharted waters.

There was no turning back now.

CHAPTER 2

Basic Training

Y ou're nothing!" the drill sergeant screamed as we stood in line to get our heads shaved. "In fact, you're lower than nothing! You're not even dogs!"

Although basic training was rough, the verbal abuse and the strenuous physical demands became routine as my body — and mind — adjusted. Still, I found it difficult to obey all the rules.

One day I showed up in formation with gum in my mouth. At the end of training that day, the sergeant came to me and said, "Steer, dig a hole six feet deep and bury your gum." It was after-hours, and I should have been polishing my shoes, showering, and getting ready for the next day. Instead, I spent hours digging that hole.

During formation the next morning, the sergeant asked, "Did you bury that gum, private?"

"Yes, Sergeant, I did."

"You look like a liar to me," he shouted. "I don't believe you. Tonight after training, I want you to dig it up and show it to me."

I thought I would die, but I never chewed gum in formation again.

About a month later (this was in 1966), I got pneumonia. The winters at Fort Leonard Wood, Missouri, can be bitterly cold.

"You better report to sick call," my buddies told me.

"No way," I said. I didn't want to be considered a sissy and get harassed by the other guys. Eventually, I became delirious with a high fever and had to be carried out of my bed to the hospital. After a couple of days, however, I was back to the old routine.

Still sick and exhausted, I was standing at attention in formation when I fell asleep and dropped my rifle. The sergeant caught it right away.

"Steer!" he shouted, "Kiss your rifle and say, 'I love my rifle. I will not drop my rifle. I love my rifle. I will not drop my rifle.'" *How ridiculous*, I thought. But I did it. During my short stay in reform school a few years earlier, I had learned that it doesn't pay to buck the system.

***

By the time I had entered high school, I was so rebellious my parents couldn't do anything with me. School was a bore, and my grades were falling. I'd sneak out of the window at night, meet my buddies, steal cars, shoplift cigarettes, be picked up by the police and hide the cigarettes in the back seat of the squad car.

I was almost crazy with rebellion. Dad would come home and scream and holler at me. I know I probably deserved it. Out of fear, I would sometimes go to bed as early as six o'clock, trying to be asleep before he came home.

I was a big shot around town; sex and girls became a way of life. No love — just physical fulfillment. I had sex with one girl all the time. When I quit going with her and started seeing other girls, she got jealous and told her girlfriend she was pregnant. She had hoped the friend would tell me, but, instead, the girl told her mother.

When she asked her about it, my ex-girlfriend told her mother that I had raped her. The police came to our house and immediately took me to jail.

In the cell next to mine was a nice kid about eight years old. Unfortunately, he had killed both of his parents with a knife while they slept.

My trial was a farce. I wasn't even allowed to testify. "We're going to hold you at the Woodview Detention Center until you are 16," I was told. "Then we'll send you to Stillwater, the state penitentiary."

As I was being transported to the detention center, one of the guards closed the handcuffs too tightly on my hands, and they turned blue. Fearing I would get gangrene, they took the handcuffs off as soon as we reached the detention center.

"You guys don't even know how to put on handcuffs," I said smartly to one of the guards. Before I knew what was happening two of them took me into the men's bathroom and beat me until I vomited. One held me while the other hit me in the guts. They really worked me over. They shaved my head and gave me army-looking clothes and tennis shoes without laces.

I can't believe this is happening, I said to myself. Sure, I had sex with the girl several times, but it certainly wasn't rape by any stretch of the imagination. If it was rape, she had raped me the first time I met her.

I thought, *This is America. I'm going to be set loose any day; they can't do this to me.*

"You guys are going to be sorry because I don't belong here," I screamed at the guards as they put me into a cell by myself. "I haven't done anything!" Of course, I should have already been in jail for a dozen other things anyway.

I had nothing. My cell was a cement slab with a mattress, a stool, and a sink. That was it! No sheets, no pillows or blankets — nothing. They fed me in a room with no silverware. If they had peas, I had peas. If they had soup, I had soup, but I had to eat it with my fingers or lap it up like a dog.

After a few days, I started to submit to the system and was eventually allowed to go out into the room to eat with the rest of the inmates. I stood at attention, walked in, sat down, and ate. Although I only spent three weeks at reform school, I learned about discipline and keeping my mouth shut.

I was given the job of stacking food in the cooler. Soon I got a few privileges. Once a week I could go out and play ping-pong. Since it was a co-ed institution, the girls and boys came together for ping-pong. At one point a colored guy and a white girl were going at it while the guards were hitting them in the backs with sticks. The place was like "animal house."

During the state inspection everything was run differently — the way they treated us, the food, the entire atmosphere. Normally, the place was a jungle, but during the inspection everything was smooth as a big lie.

As part of my rehabilitation, I was assigned to see a Swedish psychiatrist who spoke with an accent and spent hours asking me about my sex life. It was very weird — like something out of a comic book.

I played the guy along for a while, talking to him with an accent and acting as if I were crazy. It took him quite a while to realize that I was making a fool out of him. When it finally dawned on him, he was furious and cussed me with every name in the book. He hollered at the guard, "Come and get this little creep!"

Later on, at the second trial, the psychiatrist testified that I had the sex mind of a 25-year-old man. *That's pretty cool,* I thought. *And I'm only 15 years old.*

At some point, the judge found out the truth. It wasn't during the trial, but apparently the girl confessed to someone. The judge still charged me with "carnal knowledge" because I was a year older than the girl. My sentence was reduced to a one year probation. I was so thankful to be free!

When I went back to school, baldheaded and tougher than ever, my shoulders were back. I was ready to take on anybody — because I had been to reform school.

ちゃ

During Army basic training, I reminded myself of the lessons learned at Woodview and quickly submitted to the system. At the same time, my cocky attitude worked to keep me motivated. After a while, I started taking pride in my outfit. We worked hard to become the best in certain areas and earned many banners and trophies.

Those of us who had signed up to become paratroopers

enjoyed an elite status and were held up as examples for new recruits. I was now considered one of the "tough guys."

After boot camp, I went on to airborne infantry advanced training, where we received specialized training for paratroopers. Unlike regular infantry, we were qualified in many areas. We learned how to kill people in over 100 different ways, using a knife, piano wire, or our hands.

Also, I specialized in two separate modes of training: light weapons infantry and heavy weapons infantry. We were trained to be proficient with the army's arsenal, such as M14 and M16 rifles, M79 grenade launcher, XM148, 45 cal., M60 machine gun, 50 cal. machine gun, 60 and 81 MM mortar, rocket launchers, flame thrower, and M126 grenades.

The violence and hate I felt increased with such intensity that at times even I was frightened by it. This new attitude became evident after basic training when I was back home for a short leave. Some other soldiers and I were driving around with a case of Canadian whiskey in the car. We picked up three girls at a drive-in who told us, "We're having a party at our house, let's go there."

Naturally we said, "That sounds great. Sure, let's go."

The girls really wanted our case of whiskey — not us. As it turned out, it wasn't their house but a house rented by a bunch of college guys. About 15 guys and a couple of girls were partying and getting drunk.

One of our guys got rowdy and threw a whiskey bottle through the apartment window. Then things got ugly. The college guys got rough with us and cussed us out.

I went bananas and screamed, "Come on outside and fight!" They had us outnumbered, but we didn't care. We were soldiers and all psyched up. I pulled a knife on a guy, and as I did, he stuck a .38 in my stomach.

"Hey, man," I said, realizing this was no joke, "take it easy. You don't want to kill somebody."

These guys were really mad now.

As I put the knife slowly in my pocket, I apologized. "Hey, I'm sorry. I'm sorry. You guys, tell them you are sorry. We just want to go. We don't want any trouble."

Just then another guy walked out of the house with a shotgun and leveled it right on my head. By this time, I was almost sweating blood. I had a .38 in my gut and a 12-gauge pointed at my head.

"Let's go, guys, they can have the whiskey. It's not worth getting wasted over." We left, and I trembled all the way home. *Will I never learn?* I thought.

⌇

1966 — Ft. Gordan, Georgia

Airborne infantry was as close to hell as I ever want to experience. The intense training was laced with competition that turned everybody against everybody. We soon became and were treated like animals.

It was so bizarre, crazy, and yet real. I'd run around the streets screaming, "Kill, kill, kill! Kill VC! I want to be an airborne ranger, living on blood and guts and danger!"

We got perhaps four hours of sleep, and the rest of the day centered around brainwashing, calisthenics, hand-to-hand, and different types of training, including plastic explosives. Blindfolded we were trained to break down a dozen different kinds of weapons and learn the parts and how to put them together. We'd had a taste of that in basic training, but it hadn't been with the same intensity and spirit. In basic everyone was just trying to get through it and get to their AIT (Advanced Individual Training), which might be electronics, airplane maintenance, type clerk, signal corp, or some kind of education.

The sergeants who trained us lived to make us miserable. They called us the filthiest names imaginable and kicked us square in the rump for no reason. Out of the blue, they would shout, "You men, drop! Do a hundred!"

We would dive to the ground and do pushups until our arms almost gave way. To make it harder, they would put a foot on our back and push us to make us give some more.

In the barracks, the constant demand for perfection continued. Every day we cleaned the floor and buffed it with a sheepskin. In order not to damage the shine, we hopped from bed to bed instead of walking on the floor.

Our shoes and uniforms had to be impeccable. Every evening I cleaned my belt buckle inside and out using "brasso" and a Q-tip.

In formation one day, the sergeant took my belt buckle and looked on the inside of it. "Is this a cotton fiber, Steer?"

I stood breathless with my heart pounding, knowing I was in trouble. You'd have thought I shot the president. When he got done cursing and dressing me down, he made me run a mile and a half screaming at the top of my lungs, "I am a jackass. I am a jackass. I am a jackass."

The army's strategy was to eliminate the guys who couldn't take the verbal, psychological — and sometimes physical — abuse. In Vietnam, they wanted people who could stick it out no matter what happened. They needed soldiers who would take orders blindly without thinking or considering the outcome. They wanted us to react to whatever was said — and now!

One of the recruits in our outfit was a golden glove champion boxer. A sergeant found out about this and said to him, "You don't like me, do you, Sid?"

"It's not my job to like you, sergeant," Sid replied. "You're my teacher, and I will do what you tell me."

The sergeant pushed Sid and said, "But really, you don't like me do you? You hate my guts, don't you?

Finally Sid said, "Yes sergeant, I hate your guts."

"You'd like to kick my ass, wouldn't you?"

"No, sergeant. I don't want any trouble. I just want to get through this training. I don't want any trouble."

The sergeant kept pushing him.

"Well, I would like a crack at it sometime, but I'm not going to get in trouble over it," Sid admitted.

The sergeant, who was an expert in karate, said, "You follow me," and took Sid off into the woods. A short time later, he brought Sid back, carrying him over his shoulder and dropped him in front of us.

The sergeant made his point, and we all took notice.

For hand-to-hand combat training, we had to form a circle and were called out to fight each other with sticks which were padded on both ends. If the sergeant didn't like a guy, he would call him out into the middle over and over. They were always picking on somebody — if you had red hair, if you had an airborne ring, if you had a tattoo — anything to make an example of one person.

Two minutes of this kind of fighting was enough to wear anybody out. The sergeants were proficient at it. They would hit their "victim" in the groin or in the head a couple of times and then punch him down to the ground so hard the wind was knocked out of him.

"Get up, you sissy!" they would laugh as they kicked sawdust in the guy's face until he'd get up. As soon as the guy would attempt to get up, they would knock him back down. If he was someone they didn't like, they would get him in the circle and work him over.

In order not to get in trouble for beating him up, they would team one guy off with his buddy and then everyone would holler: "Kill him! Kill him!" The spirit of competition would take over, and the guy would want to kill his own buddy.

When the sarge wanted to be particularly sadistic, he would give the stick to another guy, then another guy, and still another guy. I'll never forget the day I had to fight six different guys. I was so tired and battered that I could hardly move. It was terrible.

Our training became progressively more strenuous. At times I thought I would lose my sanity. My hatred and bitterness became more complex the longer I trained.

One incident stands out most vividly in my mind. The drill involved taking a man's weapon away and disarming him. In this instance, it was his rifle which had a fixed bayonet. We were taken to a sawdust pit about 200 feet long, paired off and facing each other. A sergeant watched every two pairs. We had no more than hit the sawdust when my partner came at me like a madman screaming at the top of his voice, "Ke-yaa!."

Instantly I wanted to kill him and gave him a karate chop to his head. He yelled. Then I grabbed his hands and flipped him to the ground. I heard him scream again, but this time it was pain causing the wail. Blood was all over his face. My heart raced with excitement at the same time that fear gripped me. *I must have really hurt him,* I thought.

Suddenly, I was hit on the back. I jerked to attention as the sergeant yelled, "That's the way to do it, kill 'em. That's how you do it, boy!" Looking down at the guy in the sawdust, he bent over, cursed him, jerked him up, and said, "Get your ass over to the infirmary. Get your head sewed up and get back here fast. Do you understand me, soldier?"

"Clear, Sergeant Airborne!" was the faint reply.

My emotions were fast becoming seared. The sergeant saying, "That's the way," overshadowed any feeling of remorse or pity. Pride and arrogance swelled within mc as I pondered: *Yes, airborne isn't for the weak. It's for a real macho man like me.*

The apex of the airborne infantry training came when we had to go through an escape and evasion course in the swamp at Ft. Gordan. This simulated Vietnamese war zone included Vietnam villages, artillery fire, wire, and booby traps. The sergeants and other officers were the "Vietnamese."

After dark each man was given a map. We weren't fighting as an outfit. This was one against the Cong. Every man was out for himself. We weren't fighting together.

We'd heard a lot about what went on in the dark. Guys were getting their arms broken and even being tortured. "If you are captured," I was told, "they take you to a Vietnamese village and chain logs around your legs. Then they make you march with the logs attached."

The object was not to get caught. Although we were given blank bullets and weren't supposed to really hurt anybody, it was almost impossible not to inflict some harm or injury. Although I was scared, I was determined to get through the death-defying ten mile course without getting caught. The first guys through got a pat on the back. There were 300 of us, and all were determined to be number one.

I set my face like flint and faded into the midnight darkness. Within minutes I could hear men yelling as they were taken prisoner and herded into the waiting trucks. The "prisoners" were first taken to a camp where the "enemy" tried to get them to give more information than their name, rank, and serial number. They worked their "captives" over trying to break them.

I was about halfway through the course when suddenly from out of nowhere a lieutenant jumped up, put his rifle on my head, and said, "I've got you, soldier. You're caught."

Terror overcame me as I kicked him in the groin and hit him on the side of the face with the butt of my weapon. It was dark so I knew he couldn't identify me. I took off running like a deer. *No one will ever take me and live,* I thought. To me it was no longer a game. It was real war!

Finally I saw the lights of the lodge. I made it! I had made it! My reward was a cup of hot chocolate and a pat on the back. I was 31st to arrive out of the 300. As many as 200 were caught and taken prisoner. I felt proud of my accomplishment.

The next day at formations, most of the men looked as if they had just returned from the front lines. They had broken hands, fingers, black eyes, and bad bruises everywhere.

The lieutenant stood at attention like a statue. He never said one word about his black eye — but I sure know how he got it!

By the time I graduated from AIT, I thought I was the toughest alive. I was ready to take on anything and anybody.

I knew I had what it takes to be a paratrooper.

CHAPTER 3

Jump School

Get up, you so and so. If you can't take it, get out!" I had blacked out during an intensive run, and somebody was kicking me and screaming in my ear.

Although I had Osgood-Slatters disease in my knees and wasn't supposed to be running, I was determined to master this flaw in my physical ability. I got up and kept on running.

"I want to be an airborne ranger, living on blood and guts and danger!" All the way, every day, we screamed the same chant while running five miles before breakfast around the streets of Fort Benning, Georgia. This was in mid-1966.

By this time, I was operating on sheer grit, pure hate, and fierce competition. If it killed me, I was going to get through jump school. Many recruits, who couldn't stand the strain, had already been screened out. Those of us who had made it felt tougher and more elite.

I had thought that AIT (Advanced Individual Training) was rough until I got to jump school. AIT was a breeze compared to three weeks I was now enduring. Unlike AIT, in jump school all the trainees, including the officers who trained along with us, were treated the same — like dogs.

One day as we were running around the track, I noticed that a man was having trouble making the run. By this time, I was in pretty good shape, so I dropped back a little bit and grabbed him by the hand. When I did, I noticed he was the priest I had heard about. For some reason, he was trying to become a paratrooper. Such a feat at age 28 was quite ambitious considering the rigorous training required.

While I was in the military, I don't believe I ever met a Christian. I probably did, but no one ever told me they loved Jesus. In fact, the few preachers going through paratrooper training could tell dirty jokes as well as rest of us.

I said, "Come on, Father, we can make it." We were half-running, and I was half-dragging him.

A sergeant stopped me and called me over on the side: "Are you religious?"

"No, Sergeant, I'm not religious." That was the truth. My folks had always sent us kids to Sunday school and church, but they never went with us. Dad would give us each a dime or 15 cents to put in the church offering. To prove that we went we had to show him the church bulletin.

I would drop off the younger kids at Sunday school, take all the offering money, and go to my friend's house. It was like my place of refuge.

If I were drunk or if the police were after me, I couldn't go home so I'd run to my friend's house. His mother would hide me in the basement. When the police came knocking on the door, she would pretend not to know me.

My friend's mother lived with a big guy who had scars all over his body from knife fights. On Sunday mornings while I gambled with the church offering, he would tell us wild stories about honky-tonks and the wicked things he had done. One Sunday I won almost five dollars from him. He flew into a rage, pulled a knife on me, and threw me out of the house. My answer to the sergeant was accurate. I certainly was not religious.

⛬

"What are you doing helping that blankety-blank priest?" the sergeant now wanted to know.

"Well, I didn't stop running. I just reached back and helped him a little bit."

He cursed me and said, "I'm going to get you out of the airborne. We don't need people in the airborne like you. I'm going to see that you don't make it through."

I couldn't believe what I was hearing! My intuition told me I was in for some trouble!

The next day we were to begin our training on the swing-line trainer. After being harnessed into a big steel ring, we were to be dropped every which way, continually, from about four or five feet.

Pulleys hooked in every possible direction simulated how we would land in a parachute. If the wind blew a little wrong at the last minute, the trainee could end up landing on his head. The instructors were to tip us in every direction, and we were supposed to do a PLF (parachute landing fall).

When it was my turn in the swing-line ring, my sergeant hollered, "Hey, captain, come here. See this kid here? He's religious. He's helping the priest. Let's show him what we do to religious people."

They were always looking for somebody to use as an example. I never wanted to be that person. All of a sudden, I was "the target."

At first, they usually drop the trainee a couple of times and let him go. To me, however, they just kept doing it, and taunting and teasing, "What's the matter, don't you know how to land? You'll never be a paratrooper."

They dropped me on my head and put me in a position where I'd hit the steel rim with my chin. They worked me over, but I had determined beforehand to keep my cool. I endured it and kept my mouth shut. Finally, they let me down.

I never thought I would hear the words, "Tomorrow you jump." My heart pounded with excitement at the anticipation of the first jump. What would it be like to feel the wind rush by my cheeks and to see the ground looming at a death pace below me? Tomorrow I would know.

Breakfast was endless as the time of the jump approached.

"All right, men," the sergeant bellowed, "climb on the platform and jump."

"What's this all about?" I asked the guy standing next to me as we climbed out onto a three-foot high platform to jump. For a week we jumped off the mini platform — hundreds and hundreds of times.

Anyone who dared to say one word jumped a hundred more times. Everything must be done in mute obedience — so I jumped and jumped and jumped — no rushing wind, no free fall — no nothing! They were teaching us how to land — from the frightening height of three feet.

The next phase was more intriguing — jumping off a 30-foot trainer. When I put my harness on wrong the first time and it shifted in my crotch, I knew then this was a serious life-and-death situation.

We climbed the tower, harnessed up, and jumped. After a free fall of 12 feet, the cable that was attached to the harness grabbed and jerked as though the chute had just opened. We then rode the cable at 20 miles an hour to the ground.

The sergeants were there constantly with their bullhorns cursing each person jumping. "Get back up there. Do it again. Do it again. Watch your landing. You will break your back, you idiot."

We continually went through this process until we could jump off the platform blindfolded and do it without thinking. It's like karate or anything else; after you train over and over and over, you repeat a certain act automatically — without consciously thinking about what you are doing. It becomes instinct.

The next tower was 250 feet high. This time we were in a parachute and hoisted to the top and dropped. By then I was a little more cautious and aware of the danger involved. The sergeants refrained from too much harassment because some of the men were getting hurt.

If a wind came up and blew the jumper back into the tower, and he didn't slip right or steer that parachute properly, he would get wrapped around the steel tower. I knew I could be hurt or perhaps even killed.

In spite of the danger, it was fun because we were really parachute jumping. Again and again we jumped over and over and over. By this time we were so brainwashed, we truly thought, *Man, we're the best.*

"We're the best, and everybody else is dogs!" we bragged to one another. If we encountered a "leg" — somebody who wasn't a paratrooper — we looked down on him as if he were the scum of the earth. This kind of bravado appealed to my low self-worth. Finally, I was somebody.

⌘

Growing up, I had always been jealous of my younger brother Jerry. He was my dad's favorite — the smart one. I was the dumb one. Jerry was the one who got to take piano lessons for four years. I wanted guitar lessons, but Dad thought that was stupid. I wanted drum lessons, but that was stupid, too. Everything I wanted to do was "stupid."

Using my baby-sitting money, I bought a set of bongo drums and taught myself how to play them.

When we had house guests, Dad would have Jerry play the piano for them. I was starved for that kind of attention, but I never got it. One day when Dad had company over, I said, "Dad, I can play my bongo drums, too."

Usually he would always shut me up, but this time I was so persistent and kept interrupting: "Dad, I can play my bongo drums, too."

Finally he said, "Go get them." Since I was trying to play the drums with no accompaniment, the people were laughing at how silly this sounded. Then Dad made a complete fool out of me in front of everybody, and I thought it was on purpose. He made me feel like the lowest creature on earth — I wanted to crawl under the rug.

Although I was starved for love, Dad's rejection only intensified my hate and rebellion. And my arrogance and bad attitude drove Dad and I further apart.

I craved love from my mother, but she was too busy taking care of all six children and trying to cope with Dad and his drinking problem. She had little time to meet her own needs much less give me the emotional attention I required.

In some ways, I took out my frustration and envy on my younger brother. One day Jerry took a kitchen knife and pretended he was going to cut me. Thinking he was serious, I grabbed a knife, too. I had already been in a knife fight or two on the streets. Before I knew what happened, I had laid his lip wide open.

Fear gripped me. "Look, I'll give you money, candy, my toys, whatever I have," I promised, "but please don't tell Mom and Dad what happened." I knew they wouldn't believe me, and I'd get a terrible beating.

Jerry agreed and never told them that I had cut him.

When we were a little older, Jerry and I were ice skating on the Mississippi River along with some other kids. We had a couple of six-packs of beer and some girls with us.

After a couple of beers, Jerry started acting crazy and began to curse me. I was the tough guy in the neighborhood, and I couldn't let my little brother get away with putting me down. Twice I skated up to Jerry, grabbed him, and said, "If you don't shut up, I'm going to punch you out."

"I'm sorry, I won't do it again, John," he replied.

Then he did it again! I skated over and belted him so hard he didn't know what hit him. He fell and his head hit the ice and was knocked out for about half an hour. I wasn't scared so much about him dying as I was about what was going to happen to me if he did.

When he came to, he ran off into the woods and fell asleep on a snow bank for about an hour. I stayed there with him and tried to wake him up, but to no avail. Finally when he came to, I talked him out of telling Mom and Dad. I don't remember what it cost me, but it was probably a lot.

I was so jealous of Jerry that I was possessed with envy. It didn't seem fair that he could play the piano and know how to make pretty music. I hated him for that and desperately wanted to get Jerry in trouble.

In my twisted mind, I decided to kill myself and somehow put the guilt and blame on him. I was so lonely and so desperate for love. One day I stood on the bridge for hours wanting to jump. The only thing stopping me was my fear of going to hell.

I'm always wrong, I thought. *I'm so bad. That's why nobody likes me — I'm bad. I'm no good. Everybody tells me I'm no good, so I must not be any good,* I thought.

I didn't jump that day — not from lack of desire — but because of fear. Day after day, I was in a constant state of depression. Suicide was always on my mind.

One day I rigged up a rope on the bathroom pipes and put it around my neck. Then I tried to trick Jerry into kicking the stool out from under me. If I can get him to kick the stool, I figured, I'll have killed two birds with one stone. I will be out of the picture, and I didn't do it. I could say, "See, God, I didn't kill myself — my brother did it." Then I wouldn't go to hell. At the same time, my brother would be blamed and get into trouble with Mom and Dad.

I also liked to think that my parents would feel great remorse and mourn my passing with deep regret. "We should have been nicer to John," I imagined them saying. "Now he's gone, and it's all Jerry's fault." My main motive for self-destruction was rejection. All I wanted was love and acceptance even if I had to die to get it.

ᏃᏒ

"If you get on the plane, the only way you will get down is jumping out the door in flight — by parachute," the sarge told us. It was jump week and the day we had all been training for the past three weeks in jump school and five months in the army. Psyched up and afraid at the same time, we were ready. We had to make five jumps in one week.

Before we had boarded the airplanes, our sarge had gathered about 60 of us together and said, "Look, men, this is the day you have been waiting for. If you want to chicken out, this is the time to do it. I won't say a word. No one has to get on the plane."

I wondered how many would bail out. There were none. We were always looking for quitters and trying to force them out. In a combat situation, we certainly didn't want that kind of guy next to us. Of course, if we found somebody weaker, that made us feel more macho.

After boarding the plane, each of us tried to prepare ourselves to make the first jump. All hooked up and scared witless, I kept thinking about all the stories I had heard — like the one about the guy who landed in the tree or the one whose parachute didn't open. *In a few moments, I'll be the one standing at the open door,* I thought.

The red light started blinking, and the doors opened on both sides of the plane. A 30-man stick (line) formed nervously on each side. A jump master stood at each door to make sure whoever got to that doorway went out!

I mentally reviewed the procedure we'd learned in training. The green light comes on, and you stand in the door. You slap your hands on the door, and you're ready to go. The first jump is at five-second intervals. You go in five seconds, the next guy goes, the next guy goes, etc.

Suddenly I realized the doors had opened. We were actually going to jump. I was tenth in the stick.

"Be prepared for the prop wash," the jump master shouted above the engine's roar. "Remember, it will pick you up and throw you up and behind the plane."

Suddenly, the line started moving. I was on my way. All of the training on how to jump out of the plane proved useless because as soon as I reached the door, the sergeant gave me a shove — and I was on my way!

With a swish I was thrown up and back. The static line followed as I did a circle and started falling. The static line then ripped the chute open, and I felt the terrible jerk. I looked up and checked my canopy. It was beautiful. All my training had paid off, and suddenly I was in heaven flying by myself.

At 1,250 feet, I seemed to lose my natural consciousness. *This is God's country*, I thought. Paratroopers floated all around me — the buddies I was going to fight with and die with. It was an inspirational moment.

Then I started to remember the things I was taught. Oh yeah, I can steer this thing. I reached up and pulled my shroud lines down into me. It spilled the air out of the back of the chute, and I went shooo . . . floating to the left. It was breathtaking. "Wow!" I said out loud, as I grabbed the line another way and went in that direction. "This is out of sight." It was an incredible feeling of freedom and peace.

It's taking forever to get to the ground, I thought. Then, all of a sudden, I was a hundred feet from the dirt, and the ground was jumping up at me. I screamed, "What do I do? What do I do?" My mind went blank. I forgot everything!

Instinct kicked in, and I hit the ground and did what I was supposed to do. I had made it — my first jump!

The landing was harder than I had anticipated. I hadn't expected my knees to smash into my chin when I hit the ground. *This is really serious,* I thought. But who cares? I made it. Quickly I ran and grabbed the apex of my chute and brought it around into the wind so it wouldn't drag me.

I was not a paratrooper yet because I hadn't made five jumps, but man, I could do it! I could really do it. I was safe on the ground, and I'd made it.

In an hour or so as we were picked up, I found out that quite a few had been hurt. "Hey, John," my buddy yelled, "did you hear that Jason Hill broke his ankle?"

"That's nothing, you should have seen them carry Rick away. His back was broken," another remarked. Because of those comments and others, I started to get a little more apprehensive about jumping. Now in reality, not theory, I knew I could actually be severely hurt or even killed jumping. Regardless of these facts, I told myself, *I am going to become a paratrooper and finish my five jumps.*

The second jump was rather uneventful even though I was scared witless. The first jump had been the easiest because I hadn't known what to expect.

As the time approached for my third jump, the apprehension in me mounted. For some unknown reason my fear grew more anguished. When I approached the door of the airplane, I knew I had to jump even though everything in me said, "Don't!"

Suddenly I felt the jerks of the lines, but it was different. My parachute did a cigarette roll and did not fully open. I was slowed somewhat, but still plunging to my doom. I suddenly knew why I had been so apprehensive.

I had a reserve chute I could open, but if I did it could wrap around my main one. I knew that opening up a reserve, especially falling at 100 mph, could be tricky.

Since the reserve chute is carried in front, the lines open up in the parachutist's face. Unlike the chute in the back, the reserve is not as large. *I don't want to pull my reserve unless I absolutely have to,* I said to myself.

Suddenly, I was sitting on the canopy of another man's chute. As I grabbed his apex, I realized that both of us could be dead in a matter of minutes. Panic almost overcame me.

He began to curse, calling me every name in the book. Since I had his parachute about half dipped in the middle, I couldn't blame him. He kept hollering, "Get off my chute!"

"Man, I ain't about to get off of here," I screamed. I frantically shook my shroud lines trying to get the chute to open. Finally, it popped free. Suddenly, I was lifted off the parachute over to the side.

Before I knew what was happening, I drifted into the top of his parachute, and it collapsed around my waist. He was really cursing me now because I was all tied up in his shroud lines. At that point, however, I was his only salvation because he was going down with my parachute.

"Shut up, man" I yelled. "I'm doing all I can. Just shut up. Don't you know I'm trying? You think I like this?"

I got untangled from him about 50 feet or so above the ground when his chute fully opened. Prior to that it was about half-opened. When he got loose, he drifted right under me — which took the air out of my parachute. When that happened, I dropped like a rock.

I didn't get hurt very badly when I fell. In fact, it was a miracle that I didn't break every bone in my body. My knees hit my chin, and it felt like I had broken my jaw. "Man, you can get killed doing this stuff," I mumbled to myself.

I had two more jumps left. By this time every jump was

getting worse. Then I was thinking: *To remain on jump status I have to make at least a jump a month all the time that I'm a paratrooper. I don't know whether this is really worth it or not.*

The atmosphere was so intense, and I was so psyched up about going through it, that I didn't seriously consider not jumping again.

Whoever packs a chute puts his name and identification on that chute. Any paratrooper has the right at any time to say, "I'm not jumping with this chute." Then the guy who packs it jumps it and if there's something wrong with it, he's the one who suffers the consequences.

The joke during training was, "If your chute doesn't open, you can always come back and get another one!"

The last jump I made was an equipment jump that drove me into the ground and hammered me hard. The side of my head hit first, then the rest of me plowed into the dirt — along with all the equipment strapped on my body. I was badly bruised and sore for about a week.

With that jump I was a paratrooper — and with no broken bones. I'll never forget the thrill of standing at attention while the general pinned my wings on my uniform. I was now qualified to go into special forces or into the ranger school. But that would mean more of the same kind of training.

I was ready to go to Vietnam. I wanted to go. I was going to end the war.

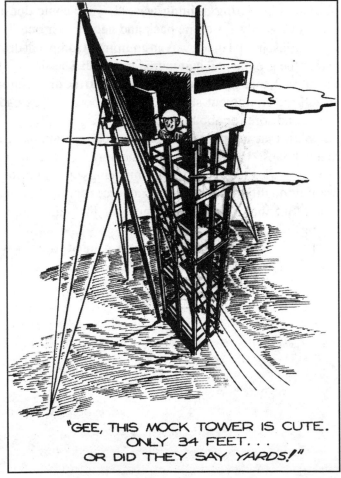

"GEE, THIS MOCK TOWER IS CUTE.
ONLY 34 FEET...
OR DID THEY SAY *YARDS!*"

CHAPTER 4

Vietnam

Before being shipped overseas, I had a few days of leave at home. Many of my relatives came to say good-bye. It was especially good to see my grandmother. For years, she had been the mainstay of our family. During the tough times, Grandmother had often brought us bags of groceries and special things for my brother and me.

In the days before I was to leave for Vietnam, I remained bitter and rebellious to the last minute. Dad was probably proud of the fact that I was a paratrooper headed for battle, but he sure wasn't going to let me know.

My mom's attitude was typical: "Johnny's going off to war!" I knew they both had high hopes that I would finally grow up. As for myself, I was anxious to get to Vietnam — but also a little afraid.

From Fort Bragg I was flown to San Francisco. It took a few days to have my paperwork cleared and get shots to ward off jungle diseases. While waiting for transit to Vietnam, I spent a lot of time drinking in the Enlisted Men's Club.

Everything was different than it had been in training. Now I was completely by myself. Buddies from my former outfit had been given orders to different places. The other guys waiting to fly out were all strangers.

Around the first of March 1967 we were finally shipped out of San Francisco on a commercial airline. Little did I know this long flight to the other side of the world would take me to a hellhole that would almost destroy my life.

"The plane will land outside of Saigon. Be ready for anything," were the words that came over the intercom.

As I looked out the window, I saw small puffs of smoke. "What do you think that is?" I asked.

Then someone yelled, "We're being mortared!" In an instant it was war, the real thing! They rushed us off the plane. Although the mortaring was no big deal, we could hear it and see the shells hitting.

The pilot wanted us to get off quickly so he could take his plane back into the air and away from danger. While we stood on the tarmac, the commercial jet screamed down the runway. Suddenly it was gone, and we were left to face God only knew what.

I was startled by the bellow of the Sergeant as he screamed, "Onto the bus — hurry, hurry, hurry. Come on, soldiers, move!"

The bus, which was OD (olive drab), had screens over the windows. "Why all the screens, Sergeant?" I asked.

"So our friends can't throw grenades in here," was his reply.

⌛

As new arrivals, we were assigned to a company and given a job — burning human refuse. The waste was unloaded into a field where we dried it, turned it over, and then burned it.

Although we went through regular inspections as we had in the States, it was impossible to maintain the same standard of cleanliness. In Nam, we learned to live with the dirt.

At first, I was told that I would be going with the 101st Airborne Division. My orders were changed, however, when the 173rd Airborne lost a few guys after a jump on Junction City 1. Replacements were needed, so I was assigned to that brigade. I didn't know anybody in that outfit and felt more alone than ever. To escape the loneliness, I often visited the enlisted men's club. I burned crap all day and drank beer at night. *Some war,* I thought.

After a week, I was assigned to jungle school and issued a weapon. On a training exercise, our class killed two Vietcong. Although I didn't personally shoot them, I still felt a sense of relief. After all, there were 100 of us and 2 of them. *These odds aren't too bad,* I thought.

I had never been more proud than the day I received my 173rd Airborne patch. Organized June 25, 1963, from the 2nd Airborne Battle Group, 503rd Infantry, our brigade inherited the proud tradition of the 503rd that had parachuted into combat on Corregidor in 1944.

Under the command of Brigadier General Ellis W. Williamson, the 173rd trained hard on its home island, Okinawa, and throughout the Asian Theater. Extensive airborne, guerrilla, and jungle warfare training in Taiwan, Korea, and Thailand brought the unit to a high pitch of readiness. It was from the many parachute exercises in Taiwan that the 173rd paratroopers became known as the "Sky Soldiers."

As the first separate brigade in the United States Army, the 173rd had to prove the validity of a new concept. Less than two years after its organization, the brigade was called upon to prove itself in combat. In May 1965, lead elements of the brigade with supporting equipment, ammunition, and supplies, departed Okinawa by aircraft. The remainder of the brigade deployed by ship two days later.

Since that time, the Sky Soldiers established an unparalleled record of firsts in the Vietnam War. The 173rd was the first army ground combat unit to arrive in Vietnam, the first to enter the Iron Triangle and the War Zones "C" and "D." The Sky Soldiers spearheaded the combat effort in the Delta and the highlands, and conducted the first joint American-Vietnamese operation.

It came as no surprise that the 173rd was chosen to make the first combat parachute assault since the Korean conflict. Even today it has earned the proud heritage it bears — the right to remain a separate brigade.

I was assigned to A Company, 2nd Battalion, 173rd Airborne Infantry. As the primary fighting force of any combat unit, the infantry battalion searches out and destroys the enemy. All other units support the infantry, and "as goes the infantry, so goes the battle."

The 173rd had three infantry battalions: the 1st, 2nd, and 4th Battalions of the 503rd Infantry. Each 750-man battalion, with supporting artillery and armor, can operate for an extended period of time as a self-sustaining unit.

The 2nd Battalion was chosen to conduct the first parachute assault of the Vietnam War. On February 22, 1967, paratroopers of the "We Try Harder" battalion jumped into combat to initiate Operation Junction City.

The 4th Battalion arrived in Vietnam on June 25, 1966, and immediately joined the 173rd Airborne Brigade. Under the command of Lieutenant Colonel Michael D. "Iron Mike" Healy, the men of the 4th Battalion came to join the fight. Since that time the "Geronimo" paratroopers have carved out a distinguished combat record.

The airborne infantryman wears two symbols of his accomplishments: the parachutist's wings and the Combat Infantryman's Badge. He is an elite and proud soldier and — let me tell you — I was one proud man!

I eventually made friends with the guys in my unit and finally began to feel like one of the boys. On our many local search and destroy missions, we learned about booby traps and the different ways the enemy fought.

Our first search and destroy missions took place close around the area. We'd kill a few of them. They'd kill a few of us. Since we had them so outnumbered and outgunned, we seldom felt threatened.

We'd be gone a few days, and then it was back to the prostitutes and booze. After a while, we were assigned larger operations that took us farther and farther away from our home base.

One day a prostitute in Bien Hoa told us, "I'll see you when you can get back."

"What do you mean, you'll see us when we get back?

We aren't going any place," I said.

"Soldier, you're leaving tomorrow for a secret mission, and you're going to jump by parachute."

We didn't know anything about that, but the next morning about 0400, we were on the airplane and issued a parachute. It was apparent that the prostitutes knew more about the war than we did.

The LRRP (long range reconnaissance patrol) was sent ahead of us, and the gooks (North Vietnamese) killed every one of them to the man when they hit the ground. An ambush had been set up right on the jump sight. They knew exactly where we were going to jump. As a result, we didn't jump.

Our unit was jockeyed around, and nearly every day we were headed for a different encounter. It was getting less and less like a game as more and more people were getting killed.

One time we were sent in on a hot LZ (landing zone) to save the Special Forces on the Black Virgin Mountains. As we ran out of the back of the helicopters, the gooks opened up on us. The entire scene was nothing but chaos. We arrived just in time to save the Special Forces from being slaughtered.

On our way back up the hill, I suddenly heard the rat-a-tat of machine-gun fire. When the guy next to me opened up with an automatic weapon, I hit the dirt! Lying in a prone position with my rifle, I was shocked when a sergeant came up behind me, kicked me in the butt, and said, "Don't you know the difference between an AK-47 and an M-60?"

Apparently, one of my own men coming behind me had opened up on a gook ahead of us. After that, I quickly learned to distinguish between friendly fire and enemy fire.

Given the command, we started running toward the battle, screaming and yelling like crazed animals. Everyone was firing into the brush. We couldn't see the enemy — we just shot. The foliage was thick in the jungle, and so was the enemy. The closer we pushed in on them, the more there were.

As the sun went down, we fought our way up the hill. Since our mission was to reach a certain point, we had to move that night. To find our way in the darkness required unusual ingenuity. In certain parts of the jungle there would be leaves on the ground that would glow in the dark. It had something to do with phosphorous. When we stuck a leaf in the helmet of the soldier ahead, we could see where he was going by following the faint glow of the leaf.

The guy pulling point led us, shooting an azimuth with his compass toward the direction we were to go. He'd walk into trees, bushes, vines as he worked his way around trying to go in that general direction. The guy behind the point soldier followed the glowing leaf attached to the back of the point man's helmet. The next guy followed the leaf in front of him. That was all we had to guide us.

Aside from the constant threat of walking into an enemy ambush, we had to carefully negotiate the jungle-covered mountains. At any moment we could slide down a hill and have to climb back up.

Every now and then, the enemy hiding in the trees would open up and fire on us. We would shoot back and hope we weren't shooting each other. In one horrible moment, I imagined all of our guys getting shot by our own men.

At times, one of our men would holler, "They're in the trees!" All night the enemy hovered around and above us. Only the darkness saved our lives.

Every time the enemy opened fire, we also fired, causing the entire area to light up. The flashes from our rifles told the enemy where to aim in the darkness, and another round would rain down on us. It was terrible. We were all scared spitless. Fighting an invisible enemy made defending ourselves nearly impossible.

At one point I grabbed two guys and said, "Dig here." We didn't have any shovels, but we had our helmets, and the three of us dug a hole. One of the guys digging with me started crying. Every time he'd start crying, they'd open up on us with automatic weapons.

Finally, I stuck my knife in his ribs and said, "I'm not getting killed for you. If you cry again, I'm going to kill you because every time you start crying, the NVA [North Vietnamese Army] open up on us."

I really meant it. I would have killed him that instant. He laid in the bottom of the hole then and whimpered quietly all night. Poor guy. But I wasn't going to let him get me killed.

That night I rubbed mud over the faces of the two new recruits. We called them "cherries." I'd already been in some combat, and it was apparent they hadn't.

When the enemy started to crawl up on our hole, I saw him coming. Although the jungle night was really black, I could see movement through the muzzle flashes.

"Don't use your rifles," I told the men. I knew the muzzle flash would show the enemy where we were.

Slowly I took a grenade from my belt, pulled the pin on it, let the spoon fly, held it as long as I dared, and then rolled it out on the top of our foxhole. I grabbed the guys by the head and yelled, "Get down!" The grenade went off right in front of our hole.

I think I killed a guy, but we never knew for sure when we had killed the enemy. If one gook was shot, the enemy would risk a couple more to drag that person off so we wouldn't know if we killed him or not.

After the battle, we found dead NVA under the leaves. Even some who were dying buried themselves so we wouldn't know if we had killed any of them or not.

When it started getting light, all fury broke loose again. The enemy was everywhere, and we blew them down out of the trees. After I shot one guy, I kept firing at him because I thought he was still alive. Finally, I knocked him at least partially out of the tree.

I realized that to keep us from knowing if we had killed them or not, the enemy had tied themselves into the trees with rags. It was all part of the psychological warfare that kept us from knowing if we had succeeded in killing the enemy.

❧

"Hurry up! Let's hustle, men!" our platoon leader shouted as we advanced up a ridge toward our main objective. Fighting our way foot by foot, we kept pushing the enemy back. When we got to one area, we were amazed to see big holes in the ground where our B-52s had dropped bombs. Immediately, we dug in and set up a perimeter.

We had just finished making camp when some young Vietnamese soldiers — about 13 to 15 years old — came toward camp. Holding their AK47 rifles over their heads, they hollered, "Choo Hoi" — "I give up."

They were down the hill a little bit from my hole. I knew we weren't supposed to take any prisoners. I didn't have to shoot them — not that I wouldn't have. Suddenly I heard shots ring out, and the boys fell like rag dolls. My stomach churned for a few moments, but then I rationalized they were probably planning to kill us. After all, General Sherman did say, "War is hell."

After we finished digging in and had built overhead cover, I set up two Claymore mines in front of my foxhole and waited.

That night, while I was pulling guard duty, I suddenly heard thud, thud, thud. I started screaming at the top of my lungs: "Incoming mortars, incoming mortars." The thud sound was the mortars coming out of the tubes.

Everybody got up and scrambled into their holes. I was with some other guys in my hole, and there really wasn't room for me, so I rolled up tight against the overhead cover for any protection I could get. Mortars were bursting all around us. It was a life-and-death situation. Some of our men did get killed.

Then I heard the enemy coming. They always seemed to know everything we were doing. They got in front of my position. As I laid next to the hole, I had two detonators (for the Claymores) in my hand. I fired them both at once.

It was dark, but the explosion cleared up a mess of jungle in front of us. I'm sure I killed some, but the next day we found blood but no bodies. They had dragged them off.

Somehow we got through the night. I could hear men crying and praying.

Ahead of us our artillery and planes started shelling and bombing. "Man, that sounds like music to my ears," I told my buddy. At the same time, however, I knew the Special Forces were still ahead of us, perhaps a couple of miles away. I imagined they were all being killed with the artillery fire. The bombing continued, and then we were ordered to move ahead.

One of the sergeants was a real coward. In fact, everybody told him so to his face. He should have been sent home because he was a nervous wreck.

One of the officers said, "We'll teach him. We'll put him on point out front." Later I found him lying on one side of a log with two dead NVA soldiers on the other side. Apparently, they fought right down to the end. Guess you could say he was murdered.

As we took the area, there was some fighting but not much. The pounding of the big guns had either wiped out the enemy or run them out. The dead — Americans and Vietnamese — were everywhere. I found the body of a friend of mine who had been dragged by a rope around the neck, then hanged, and then shot in the head.

The Special Forces were really glad to see us. After setting up a camp, we were brought some hot chow — the first in days. We had been fighting maybe a week.

By this time a new type of hate had entered us. The men would set up the dead Vietnamese bodies all around and stick cigarettes into their mouths.

One lieutenant friend of mine came running back waving a pair of ears. Showing them to me, he said, "John, I know I got this S.O.B. No doubt about it. Want one?" At times this guy acted more like an enlisted man than an officer. As our F.O. (forward observer), it was his job to call in the artillery. That night he had called in the artillery and felt he was responsible for this guy's death, so he had cut off his ears.

I had heard a lot of guys talk about taking ears, but I hadn't seen it until now. My head was spinning. *Harden up, Steer,* I told myself. *Hate the gooks, that's why you're here.*

I felt a little crazy. For some reason, the sight of dead gooks lying all around made me laugh. *I must be going mad,* I thought.

Somebody had carved the 173rd Airborne initials on an NVA soldier's forehead. I got up and stuck a cigarette I had lit up in a dead gook's lips. We ate the hot chow with dead stiffs propped up all over. It was funny and yet morbid. It was really sick, but in a few minutes it didn't bother us anymore. I was even feeding this one dead gook food. This goes to show you just how far we had been pushed — physically, mentally, and emotionally.

We went back the same way we had come — through the mountain jungle. As we were returning, I saw this little spider monkey and said, "Hey, man, that's a neat monkey."

One guy asked, "You want him?"

"Yeah," and right there I named him George after my friend. They looked a lot alike, except my monkey was better looking.

I first met George in an earlier battle when he came in on a helicopter to replace somebody who had been killed or wounded. Fresh from the States to the combat zone, he was a basket case.

When George came near me, I yelled, "Come on over here and stay in my bunker tonight, then you won't have to dig a hole before you go to bed. Since it's late, you can stay here with me."

As we began to talk, he started crying because of the scene around us. By that time, my soul had become so hardened and calloused that I couldn't sympathize with true, heartfelt human emotion. Right away I started hating him. "You're nothing but a big baby," I said, mocking his tears.

This poor kid had just come from the States and had never experienced anything like this before. Dead Americans — their bodies shot full of holes — covered the ground. Soldiers were running around with open bleeding wounds. Everything was in chaos.

Later George and I became the best of friends.

As I continued walking down through the mountain jungle, I began to hear helicopters circling overhead. "We're gonna be picked up!" someone shouted.

When it came time to board our chopper, George, the

monkey, bit my fingers almost to ribbons so I held him by his throat. He'd never been in a helicopter before and was scared to death. I tried to give him to everybody, anybody. "You want this thing? Take him."

"Heck, no, I don't want him." Nobody would take him. So I held him, almost choking him, trying to keep him from biting me. Eventually he got used to the helicopter.

After that the monkey rode on my back pack and went with me on every airborne assault. At times, however, he did get me into trouble. Like the day he decided the C.O. papers were for litter. You can guess what the C.O. thought of that!

From time to time we would smoke pot, and George would smell it, so we would give him a hit off the joint. When he got stoned, he would fall out of trees all the way to the bottom branch and then grab it with his tail.

We were a strike force, and as a result were constantly on the move. The helicopter was the workhorse of the war. We could be fighting in one place and eight hours later be a hundred miles away.

Death became commonplace, and I constantly wondered, *Will it be me or my buddy this time?* Everything became more intense. Our madness and devil-may-care attitude seemed to increase. We had lost about 30 men in the last couple of months, and the number of dead kept increasing. Two guys were blown into hamburger by land mines. Their pieces were carried out in plastic bags.

One day while tromping through the jungle, I had diarrhea so bad I couldn't go for a half hour without it running down my leg. At the same time, my clothes and shoes were wet and mildewed from the rain and humidity. My feet were rotten, and chunks of flesh were constantly breaking off. Pain had become commonplace.

We would wake up with leeches in our nose — and any place else they decided to be. Scorpions, snakes, mosquitoes, malaria, and ringworm constantly tormented us.

The bamboo poisoning on our arms had formed huge

blisters of pus. Gritting our teeth in pain, we would use sticks to scrape off the dead skin and watch the pus ooze out as we tried to wash it off.

This march was the worst. I thought I would die because of the dysentery. After I stopped and tried to clean myself up, I started out again. I was bringing up the rear of the company.

Suddenly, I realized I had lost my men. I didn't know which direction they had gone. Here I was in enemy territory in the middle of Vietnam, and I was lost — and scared.

Everyone seemed to pray a lot in Vietnam. I didn't know God, but I knew there was one. I often prayed: "Help me" here and "Help me" there, and I believe He did.

Now I was lost in the middle of the jungle. Finally, I started to remember everything I'd learned about tracking. By watching for a broken blade of grass or twig, it wouldn't be hard to follow a hundred men, the jungle was so thick and grown up. At any moment I could be ambushed. The enemy saw me, and I knew it. This was enemy territory. I might have been following them right into their base camp.

Finally, after two hours, I caught up with my company. God was with me because I didn't know if I was following the Vietnamese trail or ours! Nobody had stopped to look for me. It was every man for himself most of the time.

Later, in the same area, we came to an old Buddhist graveyard. Suddenly an old man came out with a shotgun and started firing at us. Then he disappeared.

One of the men shouted, "Man, I can't go on. I cannot go another step. I'm worn out." We were all pushed to go, go, go, and some of us felt just like giving up. So we left him there. I don't know if he caught up with us or not. If he didn't, the North Vietnamese killed him.

A couple of times we had calls for help on the radio that Australians or Americans needed help — only to find it was the enemy trying to ambush us.

World War II had Tokyo Rose, and we had Hanoi Hanna. At times during the night her voice could be heard over loudspeakers the enemy had hidden. We would hear her over and over, saying, "G.I.'s go home. You can't win this war. Your wives are shacking up with the neighbor. Some-body else has your girl. You're going to get killed. Give up. Go home. Start rebelling against this war. Have you read the papers? All the Americans are protesting the war over here. Go home you G.I.'s." Man, it made me think!

It was battle after battle, out and back, out and back. Then the word came: "We're moving up north."

One day as we were going through the jungle, we came upon an old French "burm" — a dirt perimeter pushed up by the French soldiers before us as a secure fighting area. The Vietnamese had moved in.

We'd been in the jungle several weeks this time, pushing, pressing, and going. I was delirious and sick with a high fever. I thought I had malaria.

I had recently retrieved an air mattress off a dead American. I hadn't had a mattress for a long time. *This is going to be a luxury, sleeping on something other than mud,* I told myself. My friend George came by and stepped on my air mattress. I screamed: "If you step on my air mattress again, I'll kill you." I was serious. I would have killed him. Strange how much a piece of plastic could mean to a person in the jungle.

He accepted the challenge. George wasn't one bit afraid of me. He walked right over and stepped on it again. To tell you the truth, I was sort of pleased because I didn't think George could fight. I realized he was no coward! He simply had emotions that he wasn't ashamed to hide. That's what I couldn't handle. I hid everything but my hate.

I threw a 40-pound sandbag at him and knocked him down. While he was on the ground, I came after him with both fists. He was fighting back — and I mean fighting back — when one of our own men opened up with an M-60 machine gun over us. That stopped the fight. I had more respect for George than almost anyone I knew.

Finally, I asked my platoon sergeant if I could go see the doctor because I was sick.

He said, "Okay, Steer, but don't try to pull any hanky-panky to get out of combat."

53

The doctor took one look at me and said, "Soldier, you have double pneumonia." He wired a big tag on me that said "Dust off" — which meant I was to be on the next helicopter to the hospital.

I was as pleased as could be and went back and stuck the tag in my platoon sergeant's face. He cursed me every which way, and I simply smiled because I was so glad to get out of there. While I got out, my company got hit really hard, and many were killed. Although I was relieved, I was also ashamed that I hadn't been there to help fight.

At the hospital I talked a medic into giving me a lot of codeine and stayed stoned for two days. It was nice to be away from the war — or so I thought.

My third day in the hospital at Tonsonute Air Base, the place was mortared. The enemy got close enough to shell the barracks and wiped out a lot of Air Force personnel.

During the attack, I had to help carry the wounded who were in the hospital down into the underground shelter. Then after the mortaring stopped, I carried them back up. Although the hospital wasn't hit, the area all around us suffered severe damage.

Soon it was back to the field. Back to the same old stuff — "humping the boonies," we called it. We just kept going and going and going. At times, the fatigue almost overwhelmed us, and we wouldn't always think straight.

During one of our little battles, several of us shot at the same gook. When I went over to the body and kicked off the hat, about three feet of hair fell out. We had killed a 16-year-old girl. I felt kind of rotten over that, but she would have gunned me down. She had a machine gun and was out to kill.

In the meantime, George the monkey had become mean and was too much trouble. I gave him to an Air Force guy who asked, "What do I feed him?"

"Man, you don't have to feed him. He'll steal anything he wants. Just give him a little marijuana once in a while, and he'll be all right." By this time I was smoking a little pot on occasion. When I first got to Nam, I didn't do pot because I thought everybody was a dopehead. I drank if I could get it, but booze was rare. On the other hand, marijuana was available anywhere.

Some soldiers got so high they put their lives at risk. I saw one guy lay on top of the bunker while mortars were blowing everything apart. "Man, they are so pretty I want to watch them all night," he said.

We weren't all potheads in my outfit. Some of us smoked a joint once in a while, but only a couple of guys were totally addicted. After seeing the things that I'd seen, I was glad to smoke some pot once in a while — just to forget.

The Vietnamese were superstitious and afraid of the ace of spades, so we left them on their dead bodies. This card, however, I was using as a record of friends who had died in combat.

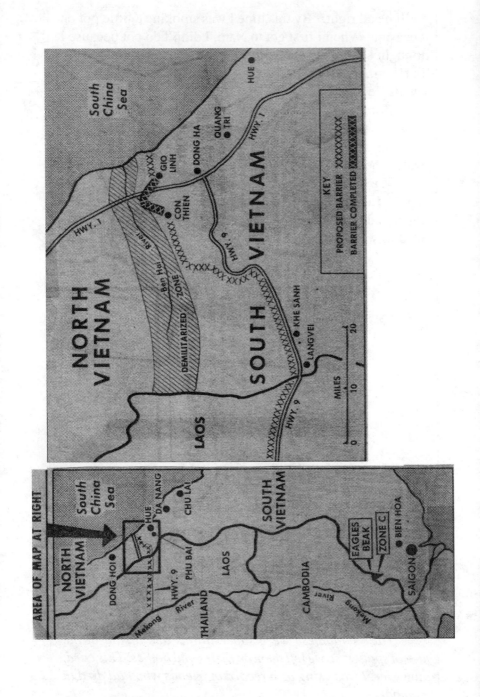

CHAPTER 5

Dak To

W e're going up north, and they don't play around up there." That was the word spreading throughout our unit.

Everybody was saying, "It's a whole different ball game from what we've been doing down here. Now we are going into the actual war. When we go up north, not many will be coming back."

We didn't believe them and said, "Right. They're just trying to psyche us up."

Soon, our entire battalion was flown to Dak To. The night before we were to move out into the jungle, a young, cocky soldier came and sat by me. To him everything was "Cool, man." Strobilsen was a good fighter and cool under pressure. He showed me photos of his mother and dad. I could tell he really loved his family. He was a sweet kid.

The next morning, word was passed down that we were going to travel on the trail. We had never done that before. With all the booby traps set up by the gooks, it was suicide.

As we walked I found twisted bamboo along the road. There were other signs also, but the captain just ignored them. As we continued down the trail, we started hearing gunfire. I was about in the center of the file and told the guys behind me: "Split and get off this trail."

Again I said, "Spread out and get off the trail."

Then the word came back that this was simply recon by fire — supposedly, our own men were shooting into suspicious-looking areas trying to draw fire. I didn't believe it, but we were ordered to go on so we kept moving. There was more firing.

The captain said, "Recon by fire. Keep going."

I knew better than that. I could hear the AK-47's and the Chinese rifles. By this time, I was familiar with the different kinds of weapons. I knew the sound of the weapons used by the North Vietnamese. These were not American, and I knew it. You couldn't see anything because it was a narrow trail. We were stretched out probably a half mile.

The captain again passed the word back: "Keep coming. Keep coming." Man, I thought it was stupid, but we were under orders and kept going. As a result the captain walked us right into an ambush. He was looking for contact and found it.

Instead of using his head and having us fall back and set up a perimeter — or sending out search and destroy squads and setting up ambushes — he marched us right into the enemy. Guys were getting slaughtered, but we kept going and going and going. Finally, we set up a simulation of a perimeter — about 40 acres — around this hill.

Since I was in weapons platoon, I was in the center of the perimeter.

"Let's mortar them!" someone shouted.

"No!" the command came back. "We might get too many air bursts hitting our own people."

As the battle continued, I was helping give plasma to the wounded. Someone hollered for someone to carry M60 ammo down to our machine gunner. I volunteered. I grabbed the box of ammunition and headed down a steep, slimy hill. Bullets were hitting all around me. I was scared!

As I was coming down the hill I had been able to see the enemy running around. Now that I was level with them, they were invisible. Many of our guys were already shot up. I was in awe of how the young soldiers stood and fought courageously though many were wounded. Many had fingers and even hands missing. I remember vividly one soldier still fighting although his jaw had been blown away.

Somebody yelled, "Steer, this guy's badly wounded. Take him with you. Carry him out of here." I threw the guy over my shoulder and went back up that slimy, slippery hill, exposed. Bullets were hitting all around me. At one point the guy I was carrying got shot again.

When I got to the top, I was still petrified. *I don't want to go back down that hill again*, I told myself. *That place is suicide.*

"The choppers need a place to land and take out the wounded," one of the lieutenants shouted. "We've got to clear out a landing area." Along with some other guys, I began cutting down the thick groves of bamboo. When I wasn't chopping, I was trying to aid the wounded.

One of my friends got shot four times in the gut. He kept encouraging the rest of us to hang on. To help ease the pain, I kept lighting him a cigarette — one after another. I hope he's alive today. He might have made it. I never knew.

One guy was so frightened that when he got shot through the hand, he went into shock and died. However, this was very rare. Ninety percent of the guys showed courage way beyond their years. I was truly proud to serve with the 173rd Airborne Infantry.

"We need an ammo bearer!" the call came again.

Someone volunteered. It was Strobilgen, the kid I had gotten to know the night before. I felt like I should have gone, but they didn't say "Steer," and I'd already been down there once. I wasn't about to volunteer again.

About that same time, American gun ships came in — helicopters with mini guns on them — firing 6,000 rounds per minute. When they came through, Strobilgen somehow was in the way, and they ripped him in half, lengthwise. He was killed by American gunfire.

I took his death hard. The guilt was overwhelming. From that point on, the spirit of suicide took hold of my life. Now I had to be first. I had to be up front. I had to be! I had to be!

Before we knew what was happening, the NVA ran a human wave attack over the wounded. They tortured some of them, and the rest they shot in the head. Over 80 men were killed from A company. We got wiped out!

What I saw that day would haunt me the rest of my life. We heard guys screaming, "Oh, God, there is nothing we can do. There is nothing we can do."

The captain was in the foxhole with his radioman, scared to death. I hated them because the C.O. had knowingly walked us into this ambush, and the R.T.O. (radioman), while checking his .45 semi-automatic after the firefight, shot a friend of mine in the knee. My friend was yelling in pain, and at the same time laughing because he knew he would now be going home.

As the fighting continued, I wondered, *Am I ever going to get off the hill alive?* Unlike most of the guys who had been shot at least once, I was still in good shape. I was determined to continue fighting.

We finally received some relief when our sister company arrived with fresh troops after fighting their way through dense jungle for hours. The enemy pulled back when they saw reinforments coming.

When the helicopters came to take us off the hill, I was one of the last to board. In fact, I wanted to be last. Part of me wanted to get killed because I felt such guilt over being alive when my friends were dead.

From the mountains two miles below the battle scene at Dak To, thousands of American soldiers had viewed the slaughter. They could see the smoke and hear the shooting, but there was nothing they could do. They couldn't get dropped in by helicopters because there was no place to land.

I later learned that R.T.O.'s (radiomen) at Dak To heard the pleas and screams for help and support, but they could do nothing. Now they live with those horrible memories.

—☙❧—

Back at Dak To, we lined up our dead comrades' backpacks — gruesome reminders of the friends who had died the day before. As we sorted through their belongings, we took any good food or weapons that were left. Personal items like pictures and letters were set aside to be sent home to their folks. The whole process was a nightmare.

"I heard they're going to send us back out there tomorrow to pick up the remains and put them in body bags," someone told me.

"You gotta be kidding!" I couldn't believe it.

"Those are the orders," he replied.

"You mean they want us to go back up there and pick up the pieces of the guys we've fought with for four and a half months — friends we had lived with — and put them in rubber bags?" I was furious.

Before leaving the battle sight, we had already picked up many of our dead buddies. The front of my shirt was still stained with blood from carrying the wounded and dead.

I had watched the helicopters filled with body bags take off after the battle. As one chopper lifted off, I saw a head roll out the doorway and fall to the ground. Apparently, a bag had come open. Someone on the ground picked it up and threw the head back onto the chopper. The thought of going back up there sickened me.

Thank God, someone in command had enough sense to change the orders, and another company was sent to retrieve what was left of our brothers.

The battle at Dak To had raised a lot of eyebrows, and military personnel were brought in to investigate the details of the encounter. They interviewed many of those involved, taking notes and compiling an extensive report.

"I heard that someone may even write a book about what happened," one of the guys told me.

Who cares? I thought. *That won't bring anybody back from the dead.*

The few of us still left were now stationed in the center of the compound and roped off from the rest of the army. Other outfits were positioned all around us. We felt like a bunch of freaks.

General Westmoreland stopped by to visit with us. He

climbed up and sat on the hood of his jeep. "You guys are the army's toughest. I can't tell you how proud I am. One hundred and thirty of you just kicked the h— out of five to eight hundred Vietnamese!"

To hear the top general of the American forces in Vietnam personally congratulating us and patting us on the back certainly gave me a sense of pride. It did little, however, to quell the fierce anger I felt. Men had died needlessly. Their deaths could have been prevented.

What a joke! I said to myself. *This is all just a facade. They're just putting on a show! It's crazy. This whole war is crazy! I hate the Vietnamese. I hate them with a passion — all of them!*

❧

"Where 'ya going?" I asked the pilot.

"Da Nang," he replied. At that point in the war, Da Nang was a secure base on the Red China sea. My only way out of Dak To and onto another base was to come in by helicopter.

"I'm going with you." I stated.

The pilot must have realized that nothing and nobody was going to stop me. Technically, I would be "absent without leave," but I didn't care. At that point I didn't care about anything. I had an abscessed tooth. My fatigues were filthy. We hadn't even been given clean fatigues yet. I was bloody and dirty — and AWOL.

After landing at Da Nang, I went straight to the NCO club. Suddenly, I was translated into another world. I couldn't believe it. Not many miles away — in Dak To — we're living like animals, sleeping in the jungle, and eating out of tin cans. I come here, and the guys are wearing stateside clothes. I felt as if I had been transported back to the States. Psychologically I couldn't handle it.

As I walked inside the club, someone asked, "Who are you? Where do you think you're going?"

"I'm coming in here, and I'm getting drunk out of my skull," I answered.

"Man, you can't come in here," one N.C.O. said, physically attempting to stop me.

Ready to fight, I switched the selector switch from safe to full auto on my XM148, which was an M16 with an M79 grenade launcher underneath.

They said, "Hey, man, anything you want."

Some older, Air Force sergeants sitting at a nearby table came over and asked, "What's going on?"

I stunk. I had long hair and hadn't shaved in four or five days. "Did you just return from the battle on the slope at Dak To?" they asked.

"Yeah, I did," I replied, "and I am real lucky to be here."

"Come join us," they insisted and bought me all the booze I could drink. Afterwards, they took me to their quarters where I was able to take a shower. I hadn't had a real shower in I don't know how long. In the jungle, a "shower" consisted of a gallon and a half of water trickling out of a little canvas bag hung up in a tree.

"Hot water!" I shouted. The water felt great — especially since my arms were still covered with bamboo poisoning. *This must be what heaven's like*, I thought.

Although the sergeants who were housing me were technically aiding and abetting a lawbreaker, they weren't concerned and did everything they could to help me. They gave me foot powder to treat the ringworm and took me to an Air Force dentist who fixed my tooth.

I stayed with them a couple of days — staying drunk the entire time. Every day I went swimming in the Red China Sea. It was so beautiful. A fence had been erected a long way out into the water. The Americans stayed on one side of the fence and the Vietnamese on the other. Not too far away on the other side were fishing boats.

"What's over there?" I asked.

"That's a Vietnamese village. We slip over there sometimes and 'get a little,' " I was told.

"Sounds good to me," I said.

That night I crawled out of the American compound on my belly through the barbed wire. The village — although fenced off — seemed to be almost a part of the base. Just on the other side, I found the whorehouse and a bar. I spent the night with a gal.

While I was at the brothel, an elderly gentleman came in and lined up his 12 children. "Pick one," he told me in his broken English. "Take a boy or a girl. You take one to the States. It will be great comfort to know one of my children is safe." All he wanted was to help one child escape this hell-torn country.

"I can't, man," I said. "I'm on my way back to the field. How can I care for a child?" What a desperate scene. It nearly broke my heart to look into the faces of those children. Before daylight, I crawled back through the American wires.

The next day I watched as the military towed an American Jeep out of that village. It was riddled with bullets and had three American corpses lying in the back. The village was full of North Vietnamese soldiers. Once again I had been spared.

Suddenly, for some reason, I began to feel guilty. *My men are back there in the field, and I'm here.* I said to myself. *I need to get back.* Somehow I got on another helicopter. I talked to different military personnel, and they got me on a helicopter heading back to Dak To.

When I arrived, I simply walked back to my area and over to my men. Everything was so disorganized that nobody realized I had been gone. For all they knew, I could have been a Russian spy. I didn't have any identification except my Geneva Convention Card.

I didn't recognize most of the faces and realized that new recruits had arrived. Most of them didn't know why I was there either.

Although they had only been in Vietnam for a week, some of the recruits patted me on the back and told me, "Hey, man, don't worry about it. We'll show you what's going on. It will be all right. Just stick with us." They didn't realize that I'd been in the country five months already. I never told them. When they discovered I was one of the few men left from the last hill, they felt foolish.

In some ways, I envied them. I longed to be that fresh-faced, naive, gung-ho rookie soldier I had been only a few months before.

But I knew I'd never be the same again.

ᘓᛮᢣ

"I hear they need a cook at the mess shack," my friend said one day in passing.

My father was a mess sergeant during the Korean War, I thought. "Really?" I asked. "I think I'll check it out."

"You gotta be kidding," he said. "Our company's getting ready to pull out."

"I know it's disgraceful for an infantry paratrooper to stoop to being a lowly cook, but I'm burned out, man."

Truth was — I was afraid to go back out in the jungle. Sure, I wanted to get revenge for all my dead buddies. But I also wanted to live to get home. Some guys were already cracking up. A couple had even killed themselves.

"Hey, man, I don't blame you," my friend replied sympathetically. "You've seen more combat and lived through it longer than most of us."

I had already received one Purple Heart, and turned one down.

That morning, I went over to the cook shack and worked all day. The mess shack was just that — a mess. The other cooks were all stoned and had acid rock music blaring in their ears.

I couldn't handle it. "I quit!" I said and went back to my men. So the one day I had to rest and get ready to move out, I worked in the mess cooking.

By this time, I had the respect of most of the men. They knew I had been around a long time. Even the lieutenants came and asked me about certain situations. It wasn't that I was so smart but because I had lived longer than most.

The army lieutenants usually were not skilled soldiers and had only been through, what we called, "90-day wonder school." Although they were just kids like the rest of us, they were given tremendous responsibility. Unfortunately, their lack of training made their job almost suicidal. We lost many lieutenants in battle. It seemed we just couldn't keep them alive.

⌘

We moved back out into the jungle again. Day after day it was one battle after another — both physically and emotionally. One guy broke his back when he fell down a mountain we were climbing.

When one of our men received a letter from his wife that she was going to leave him, he went over to his hole crying. Three or four other men were standing in the same hole writing letters.

"Get the h— out of here!" one of them shouted, cursing at the same time. "We don't need cry babies like you hanging around!"

"You guys better shut up, or I'm gonna kill you!" the distraught soldier yelled in return. Still they kept taunting him.

Suddenly, something exploded about 100 feet away from me. This guy had jumped into the hole with his buddies and pulled the pin on a grenade. These were his friends. Only one guy lived through the blast. The others were dead because of a "Dear John" letter — but it wasn't just that. It was the tension, the pressure, the curse of Vietnam.

During another small fire fight, one of our men ran toward the Vietcong screaming, "I can't take it anymore. I can't take it anymore." He went nuts, and the enemy was glad to put him out of his misery.

There was another guy who would try to kill the rest of us at night and had to be tied up in front of the C.O.'s tent. It was quite a while before we got a helicopter in to take him out of the jungle. I don't know what happened to him.

We lived on the constant brink of insanity. Most of us were borderline crazy and lived in fear of going over the edge.

Although we didn't have much contact with the enemy for several months, we were pushed hard. We'd go day and night, day and night, moving. We'd start out before light and keep pushing ahead until nightfall. Then we'd dig a hole after dark and build an overhead cover for it because we usually got mortared at night.

Around our perimeter we set trip flares out in front. At times the Vietnamese would trip a flare and light up the entire area. Usually by the time we saw them, grabbed a weapon, and got the Claymore detonator, they would be gone.

The Vietnamese always seemed to know where we were — even in the dark. They could spot the glow of a cigarette from several hundred yards. More than one soldier got his brains blown out because he thought it was safe to smoke.

By this time, all I wanted to do was kill the enemy. Boy, how I wanted to kill them. If somebody killed a Vietnamese and I didn't that day, jealousy would consume me. The war had become almost like deer hunting to me.

One day, as we moved into an area that had been pounded by B-52s, we found several Vietnamese wandering around mindlessly from concussions caused by the bombs.

"There's one," someone shouted.

"Wait a minute. Wait for me," I yelled. I didn't want anyone to shoot until I got in on it, too.

When we found a Vietnamese officer wandering around in shell shock, the three of us shot him all at once. It felt good. Killing somebody is so final. It's done, and there's nothing else you can do. It's just done!

I was filled with insane hate, and wanted revenge for all my dead friends.

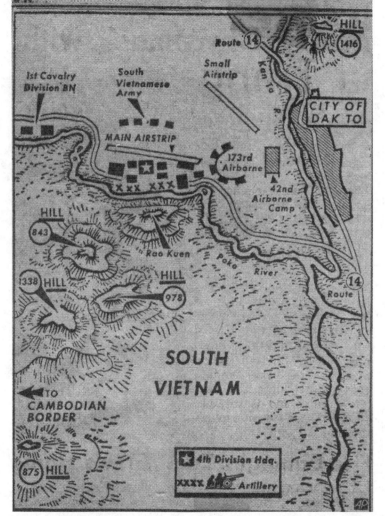

HILL
1416

Route 14

Kan To R.

CITY OF
DAK TO

Small
Airstrip

1st Cavalry
Division BN

South
Vietnamese
Army

MAIN AIRSTRIP

173rd
Airborne

42nd
Airborne
Camp

X X X X X X

HILL
843

Rao Kuen

Poko River

338 HILL

HILL
978

14
Route

SOUTH
VIETNAM

TO
CAMBODIAN
BORDER

875 HILL

★ 4th Division Hdq.
XXXX Artillery

CHAPTER 6

Hill 875

"Not many of you will be coming back." We had heard those words before, but this time we knew they meant it.

"Why?" we asked one another. "This is stupid. Why are we doing this if we're just going to be killed?"

Some replied, "For God and country."

But for me it was something else. It was revenge — crazy, hateful revenge. By this time I didn't believe I was going to get out of Vietnam alive. I had seen so many people killed. *I'm only 19,* I told myself. *I'm too young to die.*

Still there was always that hope: Maybe I won't get shot. After each battle, however, what little hope I had left was slowly deteriorating. All I could think about was going home when my time was up.

After a soldier had been in Vietnam for a year, he was sent back to the States. A few days before his one-year anniversary, he was supposed to be flown out of the battle area by helicopter. Sometimes the chopper came too late.

One really nice guy in our unit who was scheduled to be flown out had already been waiting for a week. In the meantime, he did everything he could to stay alive. For greater protection, he began to dig deep foxholes at night. But it wasn't enough. He was killed anyway.

Does anybody get to go home out of this God-forsaken

place? I often wondered. Some did, of course, and, oh, they were so happy. I would be happy to go home, too!

⌐▯☞

"You guys are going to take Hill 875," we were told by our commanding officer. "It's going to be a bloody battle, and many men will be lost."

"Didn't the Marines already take that hill?" I asked a buddy standing nearby.

"That's what I heard," he replied. "We must have given it back."

We'd taken another hill before this and had lost several men, including our company commander. As a result, several new replacements had recently joined our unit. While we needed the manpower, raw recruits always put us at a disadvantage. We couldn't count on them.

Like anything else, learning comes from day to day battle experience. If a new recruit lived long enough, he learned. If he didn't, he died.

This "hill" was more like a mountainous area covered by thick jungle. Although our planes had pounded the area, the NVA had been there so long in base camp they had lots of overhead cover. They had dug tunnels and large rooms under and all through the mountains. They had what we called spider traps — holes connected to this underground tunnel system. The entrances to the holes were camouflaged so they could pop up in front of you and kill you before you knew what had happened. It was almost impossible to find them — much less do them any harm.

Then the battle for Hill 875 began. It was November 19, 1967. By this time in the war, "A" Company was well-respected among the other units. We had a bounty on our heads, and guys only got rotated back to the States if they were seriously wounded or in body bags. Our company nickname was *no derose alfa* meaning no one survived a 12-month rotation unscathed. They were all either seriously wounded or dead.

This time we didn't have to spearhead the attack. Three

companies were ahead of us advancing up the steep hill. Our unit followed them as they engaged in contact. About 400 of us were fighting against thousands of Vietnamese dug in all through the hill.

At that point, it was like every man for himself. We were hollering and screaming and assaulting the hill. Our guys were psyched up and determined to take it.

The Vietnamese, however, were mowing men down like grass. We were wide open targets. Many men were killed, and even more were wounded.

When we finally got to what I thought was the hill, it turned out to be only a plateau, according to the maps. Fighting like crazy, we battled our way up, losing more men every few yards.

After setting up a perimeter, the men began to dig in. Before we knew what had happened, more NVA had come in behind us. We were surrounded. Suddenly, new orders were shouted from one man to another: "'A' Company go back down the hill!"

What? Why?

"We've got to cut a landing zone so the helicopters can come in and get the wounded!" someone informed us. The tropical trees in that area were too large and dense to cut down for a secure landing zone. It's ironic, but by the end of the battle most of those giant trees were blown down by mortars and bombs. It's a wonder any of us lived.

I never did understand their strategy, but apparently those in charge knew what they were doing. We fought our way back down the hill, exposing ourselves again.

This is crazy, I said to myself. But everything in Nam seemed crazy. We got down the hill and set up another perimeter; a small one — this time company size. There were maybe 70 men left out of our company of over 100.

Intelligence had information that the NVA were bringing up another regiment to our rear on the Ho Chi Minh Trail.

"Let me go back down the trail until we make contact," I volunteered. "That might slow them down, giving the rest of the company time to dig in."

Carlos Lozada, the machine gunner, and another man, Kelly, and I set up an ambush on the trail. We were well camouflaged.

Another guy from our company was walking up and down the trail with a radio headset on. "Get down, you idiot!" we shouted. Although he drifted back toward the company, he had exposed our position.

Kelly, who was off to our right flank and well-hidden, hollered, "Here they come!"

Sure enough the enemy came trotting down the center of the trail and on both sides. Every Vietnamese soldier was wearing camouflage and had burlap tied around their weapons. Their faces were blackened.

"Wait until they get real close," Carlos whispered, preparing to fire the M60 machine gun. It was my job to feed in the ammunition. I also had an XM148, which was an M16 with an M79 grenade launcher underneath.

We waited until they got close and then opened up on them. We were mowing them down. Then we realized that instead of falling back, they were moving out into the woods on both sides of the trail.

"Kill him!" Carlos shouted at me. The machine gun had jammed and an NVA soldier was right in front of me. I hadn't noticed him since I'd been focusing on the NVA farther out in front of us. When I finally saw him, he was in a prone position with an AK47. I just barely had time to squeeze off a whole clip of ammunition and ripped him up the middle.

The enemy kept coming. We got the gun working again.

"Come back in!" our company hollered. "Come in!"

"We can't!" we shouted back. "We're pinned down!" By this time the Vietnamese were starting to flank us on both sides.

"Drop back, and I'll cover you," Carlos hollered. Since I had to cross the trail to drop back, I quickly put in a new clip and started crouching backwards as fast as possible. I sprayed across the trail, trying to keep their heads down while I dropped back maybe 50 or 60 feet — which seemed more like a mile because of the dense jungle. I got behind a log and put in another clip and kept firing.

Carlos came then, firing the M60 from the hip, right in front of my field of fire. As he went over to the right side of me, walking backward, I tried to cover him. He came right around behind me and got down by the log. There was a lot of hollering going on.

"Get down lower," I yelled, grabbing him at the same time.

Suddenly, one bullet went through my arm, and one went across my back. "I'm hit!" I hollered.

When I grabbed Carlos, I realized that the same burst had just about taken his head off. I went nuts. I stood up and began cussing the enemy. My friend was killed, and the enemy was running all around us. The company was hollering at us to come in.

I couldn't get the M60 out from under Carlos. He was slumped over the machine gun. We were trained never to leave a machine gun, but I couldn't get it loose from him.

I stood up and was screaming and hollering and firing my weapon with my right arm because my left arm was useless. I started going back toward the company, and Kelly came in from the right flank and got behind me. He was helping cover me.

"Crawl faster!" he commanded and kept slapping me in the butt. As we maneuvered our way through the thick underbrush, Kelly tossed grenades behind us. Finally, we reached the company area. I didn't realize it, but my back had been split open.

George Kiortsis, one of the survivors of "A" company later told me what happened: "As you came in from the outpost with your arm dragging, you were screaming and hollering and laughing about how many NVA you killed. Then you were crying and screaming, 'They got Carlos! They got Carlos!'" I realize now that I must have gone temporarily insane.

When George reminded me of that incident, I almost fainted. Emotion overwhelmed me as I re-experienced the anger, grief, and horror I had blocked out for the past 25 years. In the official after-action report it says Spec. 4 John Steer became upset — an understatement!

Carlos Lozada later received the Congressional Medal of Honor posthumously.

༅

"Let's make a stand here and fight!" I couldn't believe what some of the guys were saying. *They must be crazier than I am,* I thought.

"There's no way we can hold them off from here," I said, suggesting we drop back to our previous position at the perimeter, where we were once dug in. I found the lieutenant in charge, and pleaded, "We've got to get back with the battalion because they're going to walk over us like ants."

"No, we'll stay," he answered.

"The h- we will." And I started pointing my weapon at them saying, "Get going." I started giving orders. It wasn't my job, but I did it anyway. I knew we'd be killed if we didn't move. "We've got to fight our way back up to the top!" I shouted. "Get going!"

One guy who was wounded but far from dead said, "Man, I can't go."

"You're a dead man if you don't," I stated, sticking my weapon in his face. "We're moving out again, right now!"

As we argued, the enemy kept assaulting and pushing forward. Guys were dropping all around us. I didn't know what was left of our company, but I knew we couldn't stay there.

Some of the guys were totally exhausted and felt they couldn't go on. Many had already been shot, but so had I.

As we headed up the hill, I dragged some of them, tried to carry others, pushed and threatened them. I was scared, but I wasn't going to let those gooks kill them. Still, I couldn't save them all. What was left of our company got back up to the secured perimeter.

I could see the fear in everyone's eyes. They had a right to be afraid. We were fighting for our lives, and we were outnumbered! Waves of gooks kept coming at us. It seemed they didn't care whether they lived or died.

We'd hear the bugles and screams, and then they'd come. All we could do was try to kill as many of them as possible and push them back. Then they'd come again.

I went around from hole to hole encouraging the men. This wasn't my job. I was not an officer — only an "acting jack" sergeant because I hadn't yet been made a hard sergeant. I wasn't even with my weapons platoon anymore, but the decisions I made were decisions concerning soldiers' lives. It wasn't my job, but someone had to do it.

We couldn't stop to go around all the bushes where our guys were shot to see whether they were still breathing or not. It's possible that we left some wounded behind, but we prayed we hadn't. We had to keep moving if any of us were going to make it. I guess that's why I threatened to kill anybody who wouldn't get up the hill.

The exhaustion and blood loss finally caught up with me, and I sat down under a tree. A rocket grenade hit close by, killing a friend of mine. There was no safe place. I could see it all happening, but I couldn't believe it was happening to me. Every time I'd do something more dangerous, I was the one who was left. It just didn't make sense.

While I was shooting, a bullet hit my weapon's forearm. It shattered and knocked the weapon out of my hands. I got another weapon. I didn't have to go far, they were all over the place.

Ammunition was dropped by parachute, but it was outside the perimeter. I guess some brave men had to go out there and get it. I was too weak. They could only bring in an armload at a time. Several of them got killed trying to get it.

Most of us didn't expect to get off that hill alive. I didn't. I was going to kill every S.O.B. out there that I could. How I hated!

They just kept picking us off. I don't know what the officers were doing, or if they were even alive. By this time plans were already being set in motion to bring more help.

I heard someone say, "When it gets dark, our airmen are going to drop parachute flares on the enemy." *Great,* I thought. *Then we'll be able to see where the gooks are hiding.*

That night as the planes passed over, we prepared to fire. Then, instead of dropping flares over the enemy, they dropped them right in the middle of our perimeter. "They've lit us up like a Christmas tree!" someone shouted, as we all dove for cover. That was just another in a long line of stupid mistakes.

Although I had lost a lot of blood, I really didn't have life-threatening wounds.

"Man, you're pale as a ghost! I'll get Father Watters!" my friend Maynard said as he drug me up next to a tree. There were about 80 wounded gathered together at the command post. Our only security was the darkness. We had no foxholes. The gooks were shooting at everybody, but there was no way we could shoot them. We couldn't even see them, but they could sure see us.

I laid down against the tree and pulled half a poncho over me. Nearby, the priest, Father Watters, was praying and giving plasma. He jumped in a hole one time and killed a couple of NVA after they killed the machine gunner. He became my friend.

At times, he said mass in the jungle while the men sat on their helmets. During the ten minute mass, if a sniper opened up on us, he would quickly say, "Mass is ended. Get out of here!" He was quite a guy. We all loved and respected him. Father Watters was a real man. (He later received the Congressional Medal of Honor posthumously.)

Later, someone told me that the parachute flares dropped by the planes also served as markers for the F-100s to drop their bombs. Suddenly, several phantom jets were in the sky over us. I could hear the screams of the bombs as they fell from the sky. Two 550-pound bombs landed in the middle of our perimeter — where all the wounded and casualties were lying. One detonated and one didn't.

Suddenly everything went blank.

I don't know how long I was out, but suddenly, even before I could open my eyes, I sensed I was dead. *Oh, God, I bet I'm in hell!* I thought. Pain and nausea pulsated through my entire body, and I felt so hot.

As I slowly opened my eyes, I saw arms, legs, heads, and bodies everywhere. I realized I had been thrown a long distance from where I had been hiding under the poncho.

Later, I realized that the tree had probably saved my life. Anyone who wasn't near the tree had been blown to pieces by the bomb. Maynard probably saved my life by dragging me under the tree.

I could now feel the blood oozing from my mouth, nose, and ears from the concussion of the bomb's blast. I started swallowing the blood like a starving man. I wanted to keep it in me, somehow thinking it would help me stay alive. I swallowed as fast as I could.

Then I heard screams of the dying all around me. *I've got to keep my eyes open and try to see what's going on,* I thought. I lifted my right arm to wipe away the blood, but I couldn't feel my hand touch my face.

Immediately, I thrust my eyes open. I couldn't believe what I saw — a bloody, ragged stump where my arm had been. "Oh, God," I cried, "my arm's been blown off."

My right leg was just hanging — it seemed by a few sinews and some skin. "My body, my body," I cried, "I'm half a man."

Then instinctively I knew I was going to die. I had no impression whatsoever that I would live. My blood was quickly being drained from my body. Soon I would be another Vietnam statistic. John Steer dies in battle. I could see it listed in our local papers.

What will Mom and Dad think? I wondered. *I love both of them so much and was never able to really tell them. Oh, Dad, I really do love you.*

Then I heard myself cry out: "God, don't let me go to hell!" It was as loud as I could scream.

Again I cried out, "God, don't let me go to hell."

I really hadn't been taught much about hell. I'd been taught some stupid junk, like: All Catholics go to hell, and all Protestants go to heaven. I had learned things like: We don't make the sign of the cross because Catholics do. That kind of religion doesn't help when you are thousands of miles from home on a forsaken battlefield crying.

I had taken two years of catechism, but I never grasped why Jesus died on the cross. I thought God was awfully stupid to put His Son on the cross. But somehow I knew right then if I died, I was going to the devil's hell. I knew it! I knew I deserved it. I knew that was where I belonged.

Again I screamed, "God, don't let me go to hell."

I passed out. When I woke up again, all my bleeding had stopped. My mouth was clean. My right arm stump was dry. My right leg, even where I was shot in the back, was no longer bleeding. It was a miracle!

I thanked God. Somehow I knew God was alive. I cried aloud, "God, I'm going to live. I'm really going to live." I knew instantly that God had heard a sin-sick and dying soldier's cry.

The gooks were going around slaughtering guys, shooting them in the head. I heard guys screaming as they were being dismembered. I called, "Somebody come and get me!" Then I realized I had better shut up — no one was around but the gooks. Still I knew I was going to live. I had met God. I KNEW I had met God!

I hadn't used my left arm for a day and a half because of the bullet holes through the top of it. Now I could use it because I had to. I didn't have the right one. I began to crawl to a better hiding place. I really don't know how far.

I found some thick underbrush and hid there. Two dead soldiers were lying nearby so I pulled them over on top of me to hide from the enemy and to help keep me warm in the cold, wet night. The bomb had blown off or shredded my clothes. I drank one of their canteens of water. I laid there with these dead Americans hiding me — hoping that the enemy wouldn't find and kill me.

CHAPTER 7

Rescued!

I felt the sun go down and watched the moon come up. Before I knew it, the sun was up again. I don't know how long I was lying there — at least two days. Passing in and out of consciousness, my entire life flashed before me. I thought and thought and thought. *I wonder if Dad will be proud of me after he hears of my death? How will Mom react? I caused them both so much trouble and had been such a jerk. Is anyone looking for me? Does anyone care?* The only sounds I heard were the occasional cries for help from another paratrooper. The loneliness of those hours was almost unbearable. I did a lot of "foxhole" talking with God. I promised, "God, I'll go to church and do any other religious thing You want me to do." I didn't know about being born again, but I knew there was a God, and He was keeping me alive.

The third day another battalion fought their way in to us. Some of them had just come from the States. When they saw what had happened, many guys got sick and started vomiting and crying. I can't blame them. American men, their bodies stinking from the rotten flesh, were covered with flies. The fire from the bomb had burned a lot of people, and the smell of still-smoldering flesh filled the air.

When I realized they were our guys, I hollered for help. "Man, don't worry," one of them said. "You'll be all right."

When they found me with the decaying men on top of

me, some were grossed out. I felt sorry for all the carnage these guys had to deal with.

"They'll put your arm back on. Don't worry about it."

I said, "You're a liar. There isn't any way they're going to put that arm back on. Give me some of that morphine."

Quickly they gave me a shot of morphine. We usually carried it on us, but I had used all mine. Then they tried to move me. "Oh, God," I screamed out. The morphine didn't do any good, and the pain was terrible. I was really cut up.

"We're taking you out of here," one of the guys told me. "In fact, you're in such bad shape, you'll be going out first."

Shots were being fired all around us. I later learned that several rescue helicopters had already been shot down. When the noise of a chopper was heard approaching, two guys wrapped me in a poncho and grabbed me like a sack of potatoes. "It's too dangerous for the chopper to land," one of them told me. Then, as the helicopter hovered six feet above ground, they quickly threw me into it.

Like a bullet, the chopper took off. High above the trees, we could see the gooks shooting at us. Two door gunners with M-60 machine guns fired continuously. The helicopter medic also had an M-16 and was running back and forth firing at the gooks below us. Two or three times he stepped on what was left of my arm. Finally, I ripped the poncho off with my left arm and let him see my stump. "If you step on it again, I'll kill you!" I shouted. Instead of being happy I was getting out of the field, I was still threatening to kill — even those who had come to save me.

Later, while in the hospital in Japan, I got a letter from the helicopter pilot saying that they took six hits that day. He wanted me to put him in for a medal. At that point, I didn't care about medals. I never answered his letter, but I used to tell people, "Give the medals to the guys who earned them — but they are all dead. They're the ones who deserve them." At that time I was so bitter I couldn't think about anybody receiving a medal in order to save somebody's life.

Now I realize that a lot of pilots wouldn't have flown into such a hot zone. After all, many choppers had been shot down before him, yet he flew one in for me. That pilot really was a hero. During the battle of Hill 875 we lost 12 choppers.

ᘒᑊᔖ

"Doc, you're not going to try to put that arm back on?" I asked the doctor as soon as he came to see me. I had been taken to a tent hospital not far away.

"My God, no, son. You already have gangrene," he answered.

"Am I going to live?"

"Yes, you're going to live. Don't worry about it."

Since then I have found that many doctors (thank God, not all) don't know how to deal with death. They'll lie to you instead of saying that you might be burning in hellfire in 20 minutes. At this forward aid station, all the doctor could do was wrap me in a bandage from my feet to my neck like a mummy and start an I.V. I was put on a larger helicopter and transported to a nearby base. Then an ambulance took me to the main hospital.

Although I'd left the battle area first, I didn't get treated first. Other guys who hadn't been taken to the tent hospital were waiting ahead of me. I was put on a shelf and left there for what seemed like forever. *Maybe they left me here to see if I am going to die while they work on the other guys first,* I wondered. *I guess that would make sense.*

Later, a fellow paratrooper told me that, indeed, that was the case. The doctors focused their efforts on the critically wounded they knew could be saved. When they did get to me, three surgeons worked for 3-1/2 hours the first time. That was the beginning of countless operations.

Two days later, when I was coming to, I was afraid to open my eyes. I said, "God, let it be a dream. Let it all be one big nightmare. Just let it be a dream, dear God." Then I opened my eyes and saw the white ceiling. A Red Cross worker who was sitting by me jumped up, and a tear streamed down her face as she said, "Welcome back, soldier."

I was afraid to look down at first, then I realized it wasn't a nightmare. My right arm was gone. "Oh, Jesus," I

JOHN STEER

cried, "it really happened." It all began coming back to me. They had a sheet stretched out from my waist down. "Have I still got my right leg, miss?" I asked.

"Yes, but it's pretty serious. They might have to amputate it," she replied.

Tears started running down my face. *I'm all finished as a man,* I thought. *Why should I feel sorry for myself? Every guy who got killed on that hill ought to get up out of the grave and kick me,* I told myself. After that, I no longer wallowed in self-pity. Instead, I thanked God for saving me.

I didn't understand it. *Why am I alive, and all those other guys are dead?* I'd seen pictures of their wives and kids that they'd shown me. I'd gotten to know them. *Why are they dead, and I'm alive?* I wondered.

The second day in the hospital I decided to write my folks a letter. With only one hand, it took some doing; but I made it. I was determined to show everyone I was tough and could function with one hand. It was the first thing I ever wrote using my left hand. At times, I would break down emotionally but would force myself to act "macho." I didn't realize how many times I had been close to death. *God has spared me, and that's that,* I thought.

༒༅

"How'd you like to be on TV?" one of the hospital staff asked me one day. "There's a camera crew here."

"Sure, bring them on. I've got plenty to tell them." I was wheeled, IV bottles and all, into the other room.

"They sent us up this stupid Hill 875, and we were outnumbered by 20 to one," I said, speaking angrily into the microphone. I then proceeded to tell them every mistake that had been made by those in command. "There were too many guys stationed in rear areas. We were out there on our own. We needed more support on this kind of operation. What makes me really mad," I blurted out, "is that people back in the States won't get behind the war. We're out here being blown to bits, and they're safe at home complaining!"

I later learned that Hill 875 was the single largest battle

fought in Vietnam, and that 287 Americans were killed.

That television tape never got out of Vietnam. It was totally censored. Somebody told me later that they'd heard me on the radio. One of the reporters had apparently recorded part of it and smuggled it out of the country.

Nov. 26

Dear mom and dad, how are you I am doing alwrite my writeing is pretty bad because I have to write with my left hand. They change my bindages and wash my wounds 3 times a day it's a pretty painful process. The food here is great. And so is the service. They will probably start opperating on my leg in about 3 or 4 days. and than my sholder. They have my right arm in traction They are trying to strech the skin over the bone. Don't worry about me I will be good as new, it will just take a little time.

Take Care God bless

P.S. Love John

tell everybody I'm thinking about them.

After about a week in Intensive Care in the Vietnam hospital, I was strong enough to travel. My condition was too serious to take me straight to the States so I was flown to Japan. On the airplane, I thought I was going to die. Every part of my body pulsated with pain.

I was one of what seemed to be hundreds arriving at the hospital. As I was waiting for I don't know what, a doctor approached me. "How are you doing, soldier?" he asked.

"Give me a shot, Doc; please give me a shot," I begged.

"Let's have a look at your arm," he said as he began pulling off the bandages covering the "stump." They were stuck to the skin and tissue with dried blood and infection.

I screamed, "You . . . mother. I'll kill you, you S.O.B." I cursed him at the top of my lungs because it hurt so bad. "God, it hurts. Oh, God, it hurts!" I lay there and cried.

For about six weeks I was scrubbed three times a day. The nurses would run the cloth right through the biggest part of my right leg, wiping out the gangrene, the dead flesh. I writhed in pain, crying and screaming at the same time.

A bullet had gone completely through my right foot. To clean it out, they had to run gauze all the way through the bullet hole. Then they brushed and scraped my back, getting all the dead flesh off of it. My chest had been burned so it also had to be regularly cleaned. After a while I was able to bear the pain. It hurt, but I could take it.

The last thing they tackled was my arm. The bone was protruding almost an inch and a half past the flesh.

These doctors and nurses were saints. I couldn't have done what they did. They were trying to keep me alive, but I fought against them because of the pain I was suffering.

In an effort to save my elbow, they didn't clip off the bone. They glued a stump sock on my arm and attached it to a traction rope, hoping my upper arm skin would stretch enough to cover the end of the stump. To battle the gangrene, they cleaned my stump three times a day, pulling back the sock and loosing the traction weights. I'd scream like a woman in the middle of hard labor. I had never heard a man scream like that, but I'd scream and sometimes pass out.

To find out which nerves were alive and which were dead, they had to pick around with tweezers. It took several people to hold me while they did it. This continued for six weeks until finally they had to clean it only once a day. During these painful procedures, they could not give me any shots. "With what we're doing to you, your system would just burn up the drugs right away, and they wouldn't help," I was told. "If we give you enough to knock you out, we wouldn't know which nerves are good and which are bad."

I became paranoid and wanted to kill them. I would have, but I couldn't because they were holding me down. I knew they were trying to help me, but that didn't stop the pain. An hour before my scrub, I would start shaking. I began borrowing dope off other patients. A lot of them were suffering, too, but their pain wasn't as intense. No one seemed to scream like I did.

Since the guys felt sorry for me, some would tell the nurse that they needed pain medication when they didn't. Then they'd give me a whole handful of the pills they had saved. It still didn't do any good. Somehow I learned to endure the painful procedures.

One morning, I was really feeling good when the doctor came in. I sat on the bed, and he said, "Steer, tomorrow we will start the surgery. We're going to try and put you back together. We want to get your arm ready for prosthesis. Your infection is nearly gone, and we want to get your leg straightened out. That will mean skin graft after skin graft."

"Okay, Doc, I am ready. Get to it," I answered. If I would have known what further torment I would have to endure, I might not have been so eager. Little did I know that good skin would be taken off of my left leg and used to cover open wounds on my right leg. Then every day acid would be used to burn a blister from the good flesh to the new graft, thus attaching the new skin to my leg. "I'm glad you're finally going to start putting me together," I said naively.

All I could think about was regaining the use of my arm and my leg. Three times a day I had to drink a high calorie malt-like drink. They were trying to put some weight back on me. I was down to 110 pounds. When I went to Vietnam I was 170 pounds of solid muscle. I had lost so much weight just from living in the jungle that I could take my index finger and my thumb and touch around the largest part of my right arm.

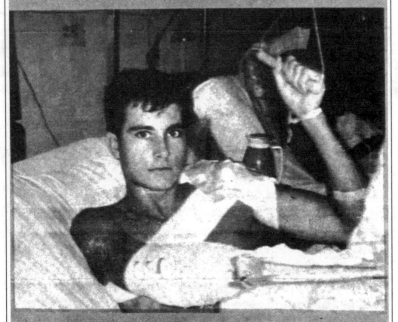

He Answered the Call

LIKE HUNDREDS of other servicemen from this area, John L. Steer of 5801 Bryant ave. N., didn't complain when he entered the service. Today, he's confined to a field hospital in Vietnam with most of his right arm missing. Steer was hit by enemy fire on Hill 875 at Dak To on Nov. 21. He was on the operating table three and one-half hours as three surgeons removed bullets from his right leg and shoulder and shrapnel from his left thigh and chest. His right arm was amputated below the elbow. Despite all this, his parents report his spirit as "good." This week, Post newspapers are printing pictures of many area servicemen, and the editors feel John L. Steer deserves page one as a typical American young man who answered the call. As Steer and all loved ones know, there are many who will never come back. To all these young men fighting for their country: WELL DONE!

The Brooklyn Center Post, Brooklyn Center, Minnesota, Thursday, December 28, 1967

CHAPTER 8

The Hook

"Give me the knife, Lombardo," I demanded. I knew Wayne wouldn't listen to anyone else. He would have killed me too, but I was his friend — a fellow comrade and also a survivor of Hill 875.

"I'm going to cut on *you* a while!" Wayne kept threatening as he backed the frightened orthopedic surgeon into a corner.

Having lost his shoulder in the battle, Wayne was in my hospital ward. Since I spent most days with my arm and leg in traction, I had plenty of time to talk with Wayne — and to think. In spite of my condition, I was still a proud paratrooper. Like Wayne, I kept my knife hidden under my pillow and most days thought I was still in Vietnam. In my mind everybody was out to get me.

In one sense, I was thankful to be alive, yet, in another, sorrow and guilt overwhelmed me. *Why am I alive and all those good guys are dead?* I asked myself over and over. *I'm no good, but I'm alive.* None of us vets ever talked about these feelings we had from the war, and that caused even more problems for us. Most vets felt that only the weak complained or hurt and they sealed everything inside where it festered like a ticking time bomb. Insane thoughts came and went, especially at night.

One evening, a couple of army truck drivers were

telling war stories. They apparently had driven over a land mine and gotten wounded.

The more they talked and bragged, the greater the anger rose within me. I didn't want to hear one more word about the war. I couldn't handle it. They had never seen the eyes of the enemy or been run over by hundreds of screaming NVA. *How many buddies did they lose?* I wondered.

"Shut up! Shut up!" I screamed. Suddenly, something inside me snapped. I went berserk and broke the ropes on my traction. To me the room became a battleground, and I wanted to kill everyone there.

Although I don't remember anything that happened, Wayne told me that I hit a nurse and a doctor and battered several people. I dragged a warrant officer who was recovering from surgery out of his bed. As a result, he had to be operated on again.

To bring me under control, the staff held me down and gave me a shot that knocked me out. They put me in bed and began bandaging all my wounds that I'd broken open during my frenzy.

Within five minutes, however, I was back on top of one of the truck drivers trying to kill him. I was given another shot — a nearly lethal dose — but something had to be done to keep me from killing myself and everybody in the room.

At night the darkness that surrounded me was almost unbearable. I thought I was living in hell. I couldn't find God anywhere. I'd wake up in the middle of the night screaming, thinking I was back in Vietnam. Over and over, I went through every fire fight I had experienced.

Every night the same gook appeared in my dreams. The odd thing was, I don't know if I had actually ever seen him. My mind was slipping, but I didn't know how to regain my sanity.

❧

Finally, I managed to get out of bed. They put lead weights on the bottom of my foot, hooking them to a pin that went through my heel. The traction was to keep all the broken and shattered bones in place.

My handicap didn't keep me from sneaking out at night and going into town to get drunk. How pitiful I must have looked, wandering the streets of Tokyo like a cripple, with only one arm and barely able to move around on crutches.

The city's lights — like a million flash cubes going off at once — mesmerized my mind while the booze deadened my emotions. All I wanted to do was forget the fact that I was a 19 year old with one arm and one good leg.

During the day, I kept myself stoned. "I'm in pain! Bring me a pain killer!" I yelled and swore until the nurses gave in and brought me an extra dose of Demerol — which I was already getting every four hours. I was a junky on prescribed medicine.

To make sure I stayed high, I paid a sergeant in the hospital to keep my water jug full of whiskey. The drugs and the booze kept me somewhat under control.

The hospital staff knew I was sneaking off base, but they all humored me. When they did threaten me, I'd fire back sarcastically, "What are you going to do? Send me to Vietnam?"

I'd been to hell and back, and they were threatening me with jail. What a joke. I was already trapped in a tormented mind and mangled body. What more could they do? I went ahead and did what I wanted.

One night the colonel over the hospital came in and said, "Steer?"

"Yes, sir," I replied.

"When you sneak out of here tonight, I want you to take the kid next to you along. He just got his leg shot off. He's really down in the dumps." I didn't realize that the colonel knew I was sneaking out. I didn't think the nurses would squeal on me.

That night, I took the kid with me to the train station where we boarded a train going to a little village near Tokyo. "Let's get drunk," I told him.

Although I didn't know where we were going, didn't have any Japanese money, and couldn't speak Japanese, I said, "Don't worry, man, we can make it!"

89

I had whiskey in one pocket and Maalox in the other to soothe my bleeding ulcer. We both got drunk and consoled one another. The next day neither of us remembered how we got back to the hospital.

⌐▮▮☞

The surgery continued, and somehow I managed to endure the trauma day by day. Fear dominated my every waking hour, along with questions such as: *What can I do with only one arm? Does anyone care? Does anyone love me? How long before I see my folks? Will Dad be proud of me?*

How I longed to be home in the good old USA. I was constantly begging the doctors, "When will I be well enough to go to the States?"

The answer was always the same: "When we think you can stand the trip home."

My drinking was becoming a serious problem, and I knew it! Nothing, however, removed the guilt of still being alive when my buddies were dead. It seemed my mind was running away with itself, and I was unable to stop it. Three or four different personalities were all striving for control of one weak and disfigured body.

I found it more and more difficult to cope, and often I didn't.

"Soon you'll be transferred to the Great Lakes Naval Hospital in Illinois," the doctor told me.

I was ready and yet somewhat afraid.

As I was taken aboard the plane on the litter, I couldn't help shedding a few tears. Why was I going home on a stretcher when so many of my buddies had been taken home in a box?

Excited about returning home, I was especially eager to see my folks. I had really missed them and realized I needed them in a special way at this time.

Although I had been at death's door and had seen the hand of God on my life, I had not changed. On the inside, I was still rebellious and full of hate.

Soon after I arrived at the hospital in Illinois, my folks came from Minneapolis to see me. I hadn't seen them for about a year and could hardly stand the suspense of waiting. What would it be like to see them? Would they be proud of me and think I had matured?

My whole being wanted to be loved, but when they got there Dad was half drunk. I'm sure it was the only way he could face me.

I recalled one of the last things he had said to me before I left for Nam: "John, Vietnam won't be any worse than what I've seen." Dad had served in the mercant marines during World War II and he had, in fact, seen Allied ships sunk by the enemy in the Atlantic.

The first thing Dad said as he put out his hand was, "How many S.O.B.'s did you kill?"

I shook his hand.

I needed hugs and kisses. I longed for the warmth and affection of a tender embrace and the words, "I love you," but my pride wouldn't let me express my true emotions. Instead I put on the tough guy image that I felt they expected.

Our conversation was bland, but that was mostly my fault. I was too proud to admit to myself, or them, that I was in need.

For the next few months at Great Lakes I went through surgery after surgery as the doctors tried to remove the infection in the end of my stump so I could be fitted for a prosthesis.

"We're sending you to Fitzsimons Hospital in Denver for more surgery," my doctors told me, "but you can go home for a few weeks in the meantime."

My folks were anxious to have me come home. Dad, God bless him, fixed up a special room for me in the basement. He went to a lot of trouble to show how much he cared, but I just couldn't express my appreciation. My heart was so hard I could barely say, "Thanks."

Before I knew it, I was saying goodbye again and on my way to the hospital in Denver.

When I was in Nam I used to pray, "Don't let me get hit in the face or my right arm." Since I had a good right upper cut, I was proud of my right arm. But that's exactly what I lost.

For some reason, however, I wasn't bitter about that. After all, I was alive and many of my friends were dead. I had only lost an arm. *So what? Why should I complain? The rest are dead.*

I didn't worry about what I was going to do without my right arm. In fact, no one allowed me to worry. My friends and the hospital staff always told me, "Man you're going to get a pension. It will be more money than you could ever make working, and we're going to give you an arm that is just great."

That sound nice, but in my mind I was thinking: *How am I going to punch somebody in the nose? How am I going to hug a woman? Who is going to be interested in this one-armed, mutilated guy?*

I had been sent to Fitzsimons to be fitted for a prosthesis (hook) and be taught how to use it. As I got to know the guys in my hospital ward, I learned that some of them had already been there for two years. Operation after operation had been necessary just to make the prosthesis fit and get a flap of protection over the bone. In my case it also took quite a while because I still had sores on my stump that required additional surgery. Also, my leg and my right foot were still weeping with infection.

Between surgeries, we were assigned to run the hospital elevators. Although the elevators were automatic, we had to ask, "What floor?" and push the buttons for the people getting on.

We felt like freaks on display for all to see. "Why do we have to do this?" we often asked those in charge.

There must have been some reason — like helping us get used to being in public or giving us a sense of usefulness — but we thought it was ridiculous and embarrassing. Some guys had no legs, and some had no arms. Others were fitted with wire braces or maneuvered about within weird contraptions. Guys with every imaginable condition were in our unit.

As a sergeant over this platoon of severely handicapped men, my job was to schedule them for elevator duty and make sure they got there. "I don't care if you guys show up for duty or not," I told them.

By that time, I had been temporarily fitted with an artificial arm. The doctors had put padding on my stump and made a mold form that fit a universal arm. After a while, I learned to use it fairly well.

In spite of our handicaps, a spirit of competition existed among the guys in our platoon. Some days we bought a case of beer and went to the public park where we tried to outdo one another.

To shock the other guys, I liked to take off my artificial arm and throw it up in the air. Then I would pull on another guy's artificial leg until it came off. People driving by the park probably thought we were crazy — and we were.

During one of our park excursions, a guy who had artificial legs bragged, "I can drive that car." He pointed to a souped-up vehicle that belonged to someone else.

"You're crazy, man," we told him. "That car isn't equipped with handicap controls." People without any feeling in an artificial leg can drive, but they need a car fitted with adaptive equipment on the steering wheel. That enables them to control the car with their hands.

This guy wouldn't listen. He maneuvered himself into the car and stepped on the gas. Suddenly, he lost control and ran over a little kid.

When he realized what had happened, he went berserk, yelling and sobbing at the same time. His mind snapped, and he had to be placed in a mental institution almost immediately. Later, he committed suicide.

"We're going to fit you for your own arm today," the

doctor told me. For the first time in months, I felt a sense of hope and excitement.

Like many of the other guys, I wanted to prove that I could do anything with my artificial limb that I had done previously with a real arm.

At the end of my hook were thick rubber bands that were used to close the hooks and clamp very tight. The bands, which control the closing pressure of the hook, were applied to the base of the hook with a spreading device. Although each added band gave more closing power, more strength was required to open the hook.

For hours every day, I practiced using my new arm. Instead of carrying the recommended four bands — which was quite a bit of strength, I carried 26! Nobody had ever carried that kind of strength. *I'm going to prove I can do this better than anybody else,* I told myself.

A young lady lieutenant who was working at the rehabilitation unit got angry at me for carrying so much strength. "Steer," she hollered at me one day, "you wear that arm more like a medal than something you're ashamed of."

She was the one ashamed of it — not me.

"Well, honey," I told her, "it is like a medal to me."

"Why is that?" she asked.

"Because all those guys who died in Nam would get up and kick my butt if they'd see me feeling sorry for myself."

To learn to use a hook takes only a couple of hours, but becoming proficient with it requires doing the same procedures over and over. My stubbornness and determination were paying off, however, as I learned to do many things using a hook that other people had never tried.

I figured out how to shuffle cards and then taught other guys who also had hooks. When I learned how to use a cigarette lighter, I showed them that technique, too. "I've never seen anybody light a cigarette lighter before with a hook," the other fellows told me.

In the years since then, I have raced motorcycles and even acquired my pilot's license.

One day I was called to the office of the colonel who

was head of Fitzsimons Hospital. "Steer, we're receiving complaints that you're wearing too much strength on your hook," the colonel said. "There's no reason for that. You are going to harm your other muscles."

"Yes, sir, there are reasons," I answered.

"What are your reasons?"

Rebellious but deliberately, I went to the corner of his office, where he had a big, high, metal wastebasket about half full of paper. Using my hook, I reached down, picked it up, and held it out.

"Nobody else in the rehab center can do this because they don't have the strength to pick it up," I said proudly.

"But you'll crush things if you've got too much strength," he replied.

I then went over to the ash tray on his desk and picked up an ash off of his cigarette. Without breaking the ash, I handed it to him. He didn't know what to say, so I left.

"A Russian battalion could go through the gate of this hospital, and the guards would salute them," I told the guys in my unit. "Last night I walked right past them in my pajamas!"

Whenever I wanted, I'd go off base without a pass. I usually went to a bar called the End Zone owned by Jim McMillian, a former football player for the Denver Broncos.

"Jim, give me a job," I begged him repeatedly.

"John, we really don't need anybody right now," was always the reply, but I knew it was because of my hook.

"Look, I really need some money," I pleaded. "Can't you give me some kind of a job?"

"Well, I suppose. If you want to, you could pull weeds around the building," he answered.

I went outside and worked on my hands and knees. For about three days I pulled weeds, doing the best I could. Although I wasn't supposed to be walking much on my leg, I finally got all the weeds pulled. I was sore all over.

After a while, Jim hired me as a night man at the door

JOHN STEER

95

to check I.D. cards to make sure the people coming in were 21 — and I was just 19!

I never went anywhere without my arm except to bed. I liked the fact that my hook impressed people, but I didn't like strangers staring at me — unless I wanted them to. If I'd go in a place and people stared at me, I'd get up and walk to their table and ask, "What's the matter with you?" Then I'd try to get them to fight.

When I finally received a pass to go home for a couple of weeks, I could hardly wait. The hospital staff had given me a big box of bandages to take along because the wounds on my legs were still not completely closed. Although the doctors had sewn them up, the sores still drained at the bottom of the scars. The skin grafts, too, were still kind of messy.

When I returned to the hospital after my leave, I went before the Army board for evaluation and was declared 100 percent disabled. The actual rating of all my disabilities added up to 150 percent. However, they only pay up to 100 percent.

John (on right) with his mom and brother Jerry.

John, 1958-59 school picture.

John in 1966, before he went to Vietnam.

John, center, with his Uncle Jim, brother Jerry, and sister Susan.

John, with two arms, digging foxhole in Vietnam, 1967.

Ken Maynard, John, and George Kiourtsis in Vietnam, 1967.

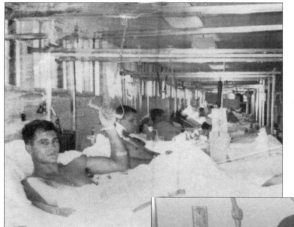

*John in hospital
ward in Japan.*

*John in Great
Lakes Naval
Hospital.*

*Aerial photo of
Ft. Steer, near
Charlotte,
Arkansas.*

Fort Steer.

The Moving Wall at Fort Steer.

POW/MIA prayer service at Ft. Steer in 1990.

John led approximately 50 Soviet World War II vets to Christ in a Russian hospital.

At the Kremlin, John received gifts from the highest-ranking officer in the USSR, the general over all land forces. Earlier, John was asked to sing and pray in the Kremlin.

John, performing with Britt Small & Festival in front of the U.S. Capitol Building, 1984, at the National Salute II to Vietnam veterans.

*John and children at the church which he and Donna
helped build in Haiti.*

John, preaching Christ to soldiers in El Salvador.

John sang to a crowd of 50,000 people in Australia.

John with wounded soldiers in El Salvadore.

Pat Robertson with John and Donna at 700 Club.

John Steer.

At the Veteran's Reunion in Frankfort,
Kentucky, John does a TV interview.

John with James Dobson after doing a national radio program.

John and Donna with Hershal Gober,
Director of Veterans Affairs.

Donna and John with Sylvia at the MGM Country Academy
Awards party in Los Angeles in 1987.

John teaches fifth graders about the American flag.

John with Barry Newman, songwriter and singer ("16 Candles"). They were performing together in a club.

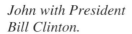

John with President Bill Clinton.

John with friend General William Westmoreland. General Westmoreland served for eight years on the advisory board at Ft. Steer.

John with President Bill Clinton.

John and Donna with Domingo Samudio (Sam the Sham) and his wife, Ann. Sam came to Ft. Steer several times to help with the veterans.

John and Donna received the 682nd Presidential Point of Light from President George Bush in 1992. It is one of our nation's highest and most prestigious awards, and was given for building and operating Fort Steer, a retreat and recovery center for veterans and their families.

Left to right: Sammy Davis, Congressional Medal of Honor recipient; John Steer; Beda Shafer, Gold Star Mother; and Britt Small.

John with two friends, Gary Wetzel (left) and Sammy Davis. Both are Congressional Medal of Honor recipients.

John, singing with Britt Small & Festival at the Reflecting Pool in Washington, D.C.

John's parents, John and Elizabeth Steer.

The Steer family (left to right): David, Donna, John, Sarah, John Jay, and Monique.

John Steer.

CHAPTER 9

Donna

I met Donna at a nightclub called "The Store." Quiet and not the talkative type, she was afraid of doing dangerous and exciting things. She wouldn't even ride horses because her folks had told her she might fall off and break her arm. Motorcycles were also out because she might get hurt in an accident.

Everything I did, however, involved danger and excitement. But wait a minute, she can tell it better than I can.

My girl friend and I had gone to "The Store" on a dare. After a while, a fellow came up to us and started talking. "I have a friend who can join us," he said. "He's been in Vietnam, lost his arm, and he's from Minnesota."

When he said, "Minnesota," I said, "I'd like to meet him — that's where I was from." Then I thought, *This poor boy's been in Vietnam and lost his arm. He probably wants sympathy.*

As soon as I was introduced to John, I could see that he didn't want any pity. The longer we talked, the more it seemed as if we had always known each other.

The fact that John had only one arm didn't bother me then — and never has in the passing years. It didn't take me long to realize he could do anything with his hook that anybody else could do with an arm. He was lighting cigarettes, flicking the lighters, opening doors — I was impressed!

After a whirlwind romance, John was discharged from the hospital. We went to Minnesota to get married. It was a big church wedding with all the trimmings.

Since John wasn't getting his VA pension yet, I went to work. When John would go for a job interview, he wouldn't be hired because of his one arm.

The days and weeks ahead consisted of one party after another — dancing, drinking, and night clubs. When I left for work, John would still be in bed. Then he'd hit the bars and play pool all day. In the evenings, John usually picked me up from work, and we'd go out to eat supper and hit the bars or nightclubs until 2:00 a.m. Then I'd go to bed and get up and go to work.

I loved him and had him up on a pedestal. In my eyes, he could do no wrong.

At night he would wake up screaming and thrashing all over the bed. Many times he tried to put his stump through the wall. One night he was dreaming he was in Vietnam and just about killed me.

Eventually, I learned how to handle the situation. As soon as I heard him beginning to have a nightmare, I would stand in the doorway and say his name softly until he finally woke up.

If I tried to shake him, he'd reach out to kill me. I knew better than to stand nearby and wake him up. I also learned never to grab him from behind because he'd turn around swinging. Since I knew these reactions resulted from his experiences in Vietnam, I wasn't afraid of him.

John simply couldn't calm down. He had to be doing something every waking moment. Even while I was pregnant, he'd pull the motorcycle out front and tell me, "Get on. We're going for a ride." We would then tear down the highway at almost a hundred miles an hour.

When I had the baby, John didn't even come to the

hospital during the delivery. I was hurt that he wasn't there, but I couldn't do anything about it. A lot of times I kept all the hurt inside of me.

After the baby was born, we moved back to the Denver area so we could be near the hospital. He started going to see a psychiatrist. The doctors wanted to admit him full-time, but he wouldn't stand for that. If he didn't feel like going, he didn't go. If he felt like going, he would, but usually he spent all day in the bar.

After Monique was born, John mostly went out alone. "I'm not going to take the baby to the bars and nightclubs," I told John. "And I'm not going to leave her with a baby sitter either."

When he had a few too many drinks under his belt, John would begin to cry. Between sobs he'd say, "Why am I alive and my friends from Vietnam are dead? I wish I were dead."

He'd cry like that, and I couldn't understand why. I couldn't understand how someone could say, "I wish I were dead."

Why wasn't he happy? I was happy — at least most of the time. My love for him was stronger than the negatives in our marriage. That was probably because I realized that John's problems stemmed from his mental anguish.

John had several jobs during this time. One night while he was at work, he had to be brought home because he was shaking and couldn't stop. He complained of a terrific headache that affected his eyesight. When he began screaming in pain, he had to be put in a padded cell and kept for ten days under heavy medication.

The first year we were married, John was in the hospital almost nine months. He had several more operations, and flairups of infections in wounds.

⌦

We didn't have any close friends except John's drinking buddies. If John went out and got drunk, I wouldn't talk to him for maybe three days. I couldn't say one word without him going into a rage.

Sometimes I would be so frustrated that I would finally say something to John. One time he wrecked the coffee table, and another time he put his fist through the door. I was so tired of him wrecking the furniture that I almost wanted him to hit me, but he never did.

I was very lonely. Although my sister lived in Denver, I couldn't confide in her because she would have called my folks in Minnesota. I didn't want them to know about the problems John and I were having.

While he was in the hospital, John became friends with another veteran. One Saturday afternoon, his friend's wife came over to visit. John had been out drinking and had just returned home that morning. I was really mad at him. This would be a good time to get even with him for the way he treated me, I decided.

When I told John I needed some pampers for Monique, my new friend offered to drive me to town to get them.

I said, "Okay," and we took off.

She suggested that we stop and have a drink.

"Okay, that would be fine," I replied.

After about four or five hours of drinking and talking, she said, "Why don't we drive into Denver and go dancing?"

"That sounds like fun," I agreed.

Although I didn't want to do it, I thought this would be a good way to get even with John. After all, I had been sitting home night after night wondering where he was and if he were dead or alive. *Now you can just sit and worry about me!* I thought as we took off for Denver. I didn't get home until 1:00 a.m.

When we walked in the door, John was furious. "Where have you been?" he asked. "I called the State Patrol, and they have been looking for you!"

Instead of taking it out on me he got real nasty with my friend. He didn't bawl me out at the time, but he was ready to punch her right there and then.

She was no shrinking violet herself and talked right back to him. "You'd better leave," I told her, "before John tries to throw you out." I knew he might do something like that.

After she left, he started yelling and screaming at me. He was furious. Instead of hitting me, he put his fist through the coffee table.

John's behavior became worse and worse.

One time while my folks were visiting, John came home after being out drinking for a couple of days. I asked, "May I go home with my folks?"

He got so mad that he put his stump through the window. I had to take him to the army hospital so he could have it sewed up. I told everybody he had walked into the window.

I began lying and making excuses for him. For five years we lived in constant turmoil. I was beginning to wonder if it would ever end.

CHAPTER 10

The Way Out

God, why am I alive? Why are my buddies dead and I'm alive? I asked myself that question over and over every day.

During this time, the migraine headaches started. To alleviate the pain, the psychiatrists started me on Mellaril, but nothing seemed to help me. I was paranoid and lived in constant fear. Whenever I met someone, I imagined that he had a gun or a grenade in his pocket — or a knife or machine gun in the trunk of his car. It was very real to me.

I thought everybody was out to kill me. If I heard a noise behind me and couldn't see the person approaching, I would go into a karate stance. My mind was always racing.

My psychiatrists — I called them head shrinkers — thought they had to swear like sailors in order to communicate with me. To make matters worse, they were both women and talked dirtier than most guys I knew in Vietnam. I guess they were trying to make me loosen up and feel at home, but their language and behavior appalled and repulsed me.

In addition to going to the psychiatrist regularly, I attended group therapy sessions where Vietnam veterans and other guys with mental problems talked about our feelings. It didn't help much.

I was taking more and more Mellaril. Soon they switched me to Valium, which was stronger. Still, the nightmares and migraine headaches continued. Eventually, I had to be hospitalized a couple of times because I was about to go blind with pain.

While in the hospital, I would scream at the doctors and follow them down the halls, begging like a whipped pup for dope to take the pain away from my head. To keep me from hurting myself, they put me in a padded room and gave me a shot of dope every four hours.

At one point, I was there for ten days. I didn't know when I came in, and I barely remember coming out.

My dad came to see me, and Donna visited me several times. But I didn't even know they had come.

I was always looking for something; forever searching, but I didn't know for what. *Why am I alive?* I wondered. I was always angry because I was alive. What I really needed to know was that there was a reason for me to be alive and that God really loved me and had a plan for my life. I needed to key in on Romans 8:28 that all things work together for good.

Although I had started receiving my Army pension, I felt guilty that Donna was working and I wasn't. To prove myself, I tried to get a job. I joined the VFW and ended up managing the bar at the VFW.

I wanted to be a cop, so I went to take the test at the police department. I passed everything until I came to the physical. They wouldn't let me take it

"You can't possibly pass the physical," the doctor told me, "so why should I give you one. To be a policeman you have to be able to apprehend a criminal."

I grabbed the doctor by his tie with my hook and jerked him up into my face.

He quickly said, "I'm sorry, man. We've got a policy, and with your hook, you can't be a policeman."

"Then why did you let me take all the exams and tests?" I shouted. "I guess you were hoping I would flunk out before I got to the physical!"

Deeper depression set in, and I started thinking: *I'm*

not a man. My wife is working, and I'm not working.

Next, I applied at the post office because I had heard that veterans were given preference. I took all their tests, and they said, "Yes, you passed. We'll give you a desk job."

I said, "I don't want a desk job. I want a route. I want to be on the street." I was still trying to prove myself.

My legs were still hurting, but I didn't consider them. I had to prove to myself that I could do anything. I decided to fight the bureaucracy and eventually won the right to have a mail route. Before long, however, all the walking proved to be too hard on my mangled leg. I quit — defeated again!

After two or three months, I started working for a junk yard, cutting up cars. At the same time, I was drinking all the time and smoking dope.

My poor wife didn't know what I was getting into next. I would bring the Hell's Angels home with me and ride my motorcycle through the house.

At one point, Donna and I even started going to a psychic church. When the people there said they could read our minds, I thought, *That's kind of neat.* We soon realized, however, that it was all phony and bordering on witchcraft.

Pretty soon I was back seeing the head shrinkers in Denver. I had hyperventilation, migraine headaches, and pain in my arms, my legs, and my back — suffering beyond belief. Most of my pain resulted from physical wounds — and going back to Vietnam every night in nightmares certainly didn't help.

When I began the day hospital program again, the psychiatrists started me out on 40 mg. of Valium. Eventually the dosage increased to the point I was taking them all the time.

I cheated on my wife, and I felt terrible about that. My psychiatrist told me, "You've got to tell your wife."

"Why?" I asked.

"To get rid of the guilt you're feeling," the head shrinker said.

To get the guilt off me, I put it on Donna. She was devastated to learn I had been running around on her.

JOHN STEER

105

While living in Denver, I became friends with a man who had been a medical doctor. He had lost his license and was performing abortions to make money. Although I thought that was horrible, it didn't stop me from working with him.

After a while, I learned that he was a big shot in the Mafia. As a doctor, he did more than abortions; he did whatever "procedures" they needed. *I'm in the big time now*, I thought.

When my gangster friend saw how quickly I got into fights, he asked me, "Steer, could you kill somebody?"

"Yeah, I could kill somebody if there were a reason, sure."

"What if somebody was coming against our organization. We're just trying to be decent people and sell dope and stuff. What about that?"

"For a price I could kill . . . sure."

"Steer," he said, "I have some important men I want you to meet. With me you are going places. You can make a lot of money. You can do good."

He set up a meeting with the "big guys" and told me, "You've got a big mouth. When you go in there, just keep it shut. I'll do all the talking. You just shut up."

We met three or four guys at the Paddock Lounge on West Colfax and talked about a "contract" on some guy they wanted to eliminate.

A few days later, however, I met some other guys in another town — actually they were drunks like me. We began hanging around together and I never went back to see my doctor friend again.

ᚱ᚜

I went from one job to another, but nothing satisfied me. After dragging Donna all over the country, we finally bought a house and five acres near Longmont, Colorado. We fixed it up and raised some hogs and 200 rabbits.

When I'd bring people to the house, I'd call Donna

filthy names and treat her like dirt. I don't know why, because I loved her.

By this time I wanted to quit drinking, but I couldn't. Every once in a while I would start shaking and unable to control myself. At that point, Donna would take me to the hospital, and they'd shoot me full of dope (thorizine).

One day I received a letter from my Aunt Elaine, telling us about Arkansas. I'd been through there as a kid, so I told Donna, "Let's go to Arkansas. It's really beautiful there."

"But we've just settled into our new house, Donna said. "Besides, we don't know anybody in Arkansas."

"Well, I have an aunt and uncle there. Let's sell this and go to Arkansas." We found a 40-acre farm and bought it. Within three or four months we moved to Arkansas.

At the time, I didn't realize we had moved to a dry county. "I would never have bought this place if I'd known I had to drive 40 miles to get a drink," I said to myself.

To make matters worse, I couldn't get anybody to go with me to get the booze. That's when I started bootlegging.

Not long after we settled in Arkansas, I got into a fight with a big guy in town. I broke his nose and bloodied up his face. For some reason, I always felt I had to prove myself. My greatest fear was that people would find out I didn't know anything. To escape my feelings of inferiority and inadequacy, I stayed drunk all the time.

Sometimes when I came home after a night of drinking, I might mention to Donna that I was supposed to go fishing the next day or do something. The next morning when I woke up, however, I wouldn't remember. Realizing that I needed help, I trained Donna to write down whatever I said. That made it possible for me to function fairly well as an alcoholic.

The drinking, however, could not relieve the mental and spiritual anguish that tormented me day after day. To escape the pain, I often did things that bordered on the suicidal. Wherever I went, I drove a hundred miles an hour. In one year, I wrecked three trucks.

By this time, I had been out of the service for five years. Five years of the same lies — just different places.

One day a telephone lineman was working on the telephone pole at the farm. For some reason, he asked me, "Are you a Christian?"

"Yeah, sure. God brought me through Vietnam. I'll always remember God," I answered. Although a seed was planted in my heart that day, my life continued on a downward spiral.

By this time, my body was beginning to show the effects of all the abuse I had imposed on it. The doctors told me that I had black spots on my lungs. No wonder, I was smoking four packs of cigarettes a day. In addition, I was drinking as much booze as I could consume and eating Valium like candy.

I had arranged with the doctor that when I needed extra medication, Donna could take me to the hospital where I'd be given a bag of syringes filled with Demerol. I'd go home and shoot it in my leg.

My mind was shutting down. Most of the time I couldn't tell you what day it was, and I didn't care.

I laid awake one whole night and cried out to God saying, "God, I want to kill myself. My daughter is epileptic. I've made my wife's life miserable. I'm miserable. If this is all there is to life, I want to die."

Monique, our daughter, was an epileptic, taking double the maximum doses of Phenobarbital. At two years old, she was a drug addict who couldn't even walk, except from furniture to furniture because of the effect the drugs had on her.

"It's my fault she's like this," I told God and blamed myself for Monique's condition. "Please, let me die!"

I was still afraid to commit suicide because I thought I'd end up in hell. Part of me wanted to think I could con God and slip into eternity in a fatal car accident — but I knew it wouldn't work that way.

The next morning, I decided, I'm through drinking and smoking and doing dope. I kept taking the Valium because

I told myself, *That's medicine, and I need it.* Eventually, I flushed 580 pills down the toilet. Without my artificial stimulants, I began to go through withdrawal symptoms. I was so miserable I cursed my wife. Oh, how I cursed Donna.

"Why don't you leave me?" I pleaded. "Get out of here! I don't want you to see me like this." When Donna tried to help me, it only made me feel worse. She was so good. I knew I didn't deserve her.

***

That night was a turning point for me. I realize now that many people must have been praying for me.

I started searching for God. Donna and I began attending the Baptist church. But all I got was religion along with a spirit of self-righteousness.

When my drinking buddies found out I'd "got religion," they wouldn't come around any longer.

I'd tell them, "Bring your booze and come out to the house. We can play some pool." But they refused to come.

At the Baptist church they preached that a person had to accept Jesus Christ as Saviour. I knew God, but I had never thought much about Jesus.

One Sunday I went forward to the altar and prayed, "Jesus, I accept You as my Saviour. Forgive me my sins." Nothing happened. No wonder. I was just mouthing words. My heart had not been changed. I got up off my knees, and people patted me on the back. But I didn't believe God heard me.

I thought, *Maybe I've got to get baptized.* Many showed up to see the local bootlegger get baptized. So I was baptized. Nothing happened — or at least it didn't seem so to me.

I was getting more and more frustrated at my attempts to be religious. *I'm losing so much,* I told myself. *I don't have my dope, and I'm still having withdrawals. I really want to do right in my heart, but I can't seem to make it — why try?*

One Sunday the pastor at the little Baptist church said, "We believe this book from cover to cover," as he held up the Holy Bible.

Something hit me. If I really wanted to find God, I needed to believe His Word — all of it. Whether I agreed with it or not, I had to believe it. I said to Donna, "I'm going to read the Bible and believe it all, even though I don't understand it."

In the midst of this struggle, God sent a man to me. Bill, who was a few years older, came to the house one day and said, "Hey, I heard you're a Christian."

My attitude was, "If there ever was a Christian, that's me." I was just going along doing my good works and trying to be religious.

Bill told me, "John, you need to have a personal relationship with Jesus Christ," and showed me verses in the Bible.

I said, "That's crazy."

But the Spirit of the Lord was talking to me: "You said you were going to believe it all."

Bill left, but he kept coming back, planting seeds of faith in my heart.

During this time, I was still miserable. *I'm religious, and I'm miserable,* I thought. *I've lost my friends. I'm still having nightmares. I'm still sitting up until the last television show goes off the air — afraid to go to bed because I know I will have a bad dream.*

"What am I supposed to do?" I cried out.

Bill kept coming back. "I want to see John," he'd tell Donna.

"Tell him I'm sick," I'd moan.

He didn't care. "I'd better come in and pray for him," he'd say as he pushed his way into the house to pray for me.

Finally I started liking him a little. I even went to his house a couple of times to talk with him.

Then Bill started coming to the house every day, and he was driving me nuts. He'd follow me around, showing me Scriptures, while I was trying to get away from him. He wouldn't let me go. "John," he asked, "are you reading the Word?"

"Well, when I read, my eyes water up, and I can't see

anything." I had better than 20-20 vision because I went to the doctor and had my eyes checked. "Every time I pick up a Bible my eyes water and get red, making it impossible for me to see. When I read anything else, I don't have any eye problems — only when I try to read the Bible."

"I've got an idea," Bill said. The next day he brought me the entire Bible on records along with his record player. Bill showed me he loved me and that it didn't matter who I was or what I had become.

Away from the house, we had a building that I had used for my bootlegging operation. It had a juke box and a pool table. After Bill gave me the records, I would shoot pool all night, listen to the Bible, and finally collapse into bed from exhaustion.

The first month I went through the whole Bible twice — 76 hours of it. God would quicken a different Scripture every time I listened. Although I was wrestling with the power of the Word, faith began to build in me.

God's Word eventually worked on me until I said, "I'm really going to give Christ a chance. I am going to surrender everything to God." I didn't want anybody to see me praying, so I locked the doors and prayed for what seemed to be hours.

During this time, I was still going to the Baptist church. Although I was leading the choir and active in the church, it was all a phony facade.

They say they know they're saved, I told myself, *but they must be lying. If they aren't lying, I want to find out what they have.* My problem was that I had never repented.

Two nights in a row I got down on my knees, shut the lights off, locked the door, pulled the curtains in my little building, and prayed, "God if You are real, if there is really something to this Christianity thing, reveal yourself to me tonight!"

Nothing happened, and I felt like a thousand people were laughing at me. I felt terrible. In frustration, I'd smash the balls around the table, but the Word was still playing. Those Bible records were always going — the Word, the Word.

The next night, I did the same thing and smashed the balls again. *I'm ready to forget this whole religious mess*, I said to myself. *This is ridiculous. I'm making a fool of myself.* I wanted to give up.

⌇

One night at 10 p.m., I got a phone call from Bill. He said, "John, do you believe in praying for the sick?"

Then I recalled that God delivered me from Vietnam. I also remembered all the Scriptures I'd been hearing from the Bible about Jesus healing people. I answered, "Yes, I guess so."

"Well, John, my little girl is really sick. Would you come over and pray for her?"

I thought, *This guy's a little dingy.* Since Bill was pentecostal, I knew he believed in healing and the power of the Holy Spirit.

Before I knew what had happened, I said, "Sure, Bill, I'll come over," and hung up the phone.

I turned to Donna and said, "Honey, Bill wants me to come and pray with him for his little girl. She's sick. He said something about some ritual of laying on hands. I don't know what he's going to do, but I'm going to go and make sure that he takes her to the hospital afterwards."

That was my motive for going: to make sure he didn't let that little girl die. My heart was seeking God, so I was willing to do anything.

When I got to the house, his little girl was lying on the couch. I felt her head, and she was burning up with fever.

I didn't know about this laying on of hands business, so I asked, "Bill, what do we do?"

"Put your hand on her."

"Where?"

"Just put your hand on her head and ask the Lord to heal her."

So I prayed as Bill had instructed, not really expecting anything. Her fever broke under my fingertips, and she became cool.

As I felt the presence of the Lord, something happened in me. For the first time in my life, I saw myself through God's eyes. I was unclean. Always before I had justified myself.

I would say to my wife, "If you think I'm a drunk, I don't drink nearly as much as so-and-so down the street. You think I get in a lot of fights — you should meet my friend over here, he gets in a lot more fights than I do." I would always justify myself. But for the first time in my life I felt terribly unclean next to God.

I need a Saviour, I thought. God's presence in that room humbled me and knocked all the props out. I had always been taught that a person has to be good to go to heaven. Suddenly, I realized that next to Jesus no one is good.

Bill had been teaching me that I needed to be saved and accept Jesus. "Do you want to make a commitment to the Lord?" Bill asked me.

"Yes," I replied and bowed my head. As Bill and his wife prayed for me, demon spirits began to manifest themselves. Using my mouth, the demons began to curse God in what sounded like Vietnamese or some other Oriental language. I began shaking violently and screaming at God.

Bill and his wife boldly rebuked the demons and commanded, "Come out of him in the name of Jesus!"

Since I didn't understand what was happening, I was saying to myself, *How can I come out of me in the name of Jesus? I'm going crazy again — I'm going to end up in the mental ward.* I was scared to death.

As they continued to pray with me, I began to feel that something within me had changed. I felt empty.

The Scripture says, "When the room was swept and garnished the demons come out, they go into the earth seeking, and come back with seven more wicked than themselves" (Matt. 12:43–45).

At that point, my mind and body were totally empty. I wondered, *Which is worse? Being demon-possessed or empty?* At least when I was demon-possessed, I thought I was Mr. Cool and capable of handling any situation. At least

I had my wit and experience and might.

Now I was empty and realized I was nothing. I felt like a bug that anyone could easily step on and destroy. As I sat in the middle of the room feeling totally empty, I looked at the door and wanted to run for it.

As Bill and his wife continued to pray for me, I thought, *This is crazy. These people are religious nuts, and I'm not sure about what's going on — but it's pretty scary.*

Finally, I got up and went to the other side of the room to be by myself. I got down on my knees and prayed. "God, I want you to be real to me, but how do I know that you're real?" I asked. "How do I know that this is not just a bunch of hocus-pocus?"

The Lord reminded me of the times I should have been killed — when a drunken college student was holding a shotgun on my stomach and another guy was holding a .38 on my head. The Lord reminded me of the times I should have died in Vietnam. All these things flashed before my mind.

The Lord was speaking to my heart: "Trust Me, trust Me."

Finally, I prayed, "God, I'm going to yield myself to You." When I did, I fell right down on my face. I can't explain it. I was "out" in the Spirit and surrounded by warmth, lights, and beautiful music. I was aware of other people in the room, but I didn't want to do anything to spoil that moment. I thought, *It's too bad they're not here with me.*

As a lay on the floor, the Lord delivered me. All the hatred and anger that was inside of me drained away and was replaced with His love. My life was completely changed.

Although I had quit drinking and doing drugs and smoking a couple of weeks earlier, it had been a tremendous struggle. Suddenly, however, the desire for those things was taken away. I realized that being saved was not a matter of doing the right things and avoiding the wrong. It meant being changed from the inside out.

Suddenly, I was a new person — a new creature in Christ! I had invited Jesus into my life and experienced an inner cleansing. I now had a personal relationship with Jesus Christ. I was truly born again.

I know that salvation is a matter of faith and confession, as God's Word says: "If we confess with our mouth and believe with our heart that God raised Jesus from the dead, we will be saved" (Rom. 10:9–10).

Not everyone has such a dramatic salvation experience as I had. Jesus deals with each of us on a personal level and meets us at our particular point of need. I was hurting and suffering so much that I needed that to be clean.

I rushed home to Donna and shouted, "Honey, you won't believe this. There really is a Jesus. I got saved, and I know it. Jesus lives in me."

She was so afraid. She'd seen me crazy before.

"Honey, you've got to experience Jesus like I just did. Let's pray," I urged.

"I'm a Catholic, and I go to a Baptist church with you. Isn't that enough?" she asked.

Within a few days Donna, too, had a wonderful experience with the Lord. She, also, was then born again.

⇒ ❚ ⇐

Not long after we were saved, Donna and I were driving our daughter to the Air Force Hospital. Monique was having four epileptic seizures a day and taking double the maximum dose of Phenobarbital. Every month she had to have an EEG because she also had brain damage. The doctors were trying to control the seizures, but so far they had been unsuccessful.

Suddenly I realized, "If God can touch me, He can touch Monique. Let's pray for her." Donna and I both said a silent prayer in the truck before entering the hospital.

Monique had been assigned to a new doctor because they were going to put her on a new program of drugs. After the doctor ran the EEG, he came out and simply said, "It's gone. It's all cleared up — it's gone." He then added, "Quit giving her the medicine."

The other doctors had told Donna and I that Monique would need help withdrawing from her present medicine.

"Doctor, are you certain we shouldn't give her drugs to make it easier on her?" I questioned.

"I'm certain," was his reply.

From that day she has never had another seizure or any withdrawal symptoms from the medication.

I, too, am free from fear, pills, booze, and the other crutches I had clung to for life. My walk with Jesus has removed the hate and bitterness from my heart. Today my family serves Jesus full-time — bringing hope and joy to those who have none.

Jesus indeed came into this world to set the captives free and heal the wounded soldier.

CHAPTER 11

New Friends

I didn't make new Christian friends right away, so I'd go see my buddies in town. They'd be standing around telling dirty jokes and passing around a pint of whiskey. I thought, *Well, they're still my friends.*

When I'd arrive on the scene, however, the conversation would change. They wouldn't talk about the same things and seemed to feel uncomfortable around me. I'd say, "Why don't you guys come up to the house and shoot pool?"

They would always give me some kind of excuse. Finally, they did come and brought a whole carton of booze. They did everything but try to pour it down me.

"I don't want it!" I tried to explain. "I'm not trying to be religious — I just don't want that stuff anymore!"

Later, I shared Jesus with them. One of the men told the rest of the guys, "I think there's really something different about him. Leave him alone. Leave him alone!"

After they left, I complained to God, "I know my life has changed and everything is better, but now I don't have any friends."

I realize now that these guys were not really my friends. In a barroom fight, they might have risked their life for me, but only if they were drunk — like we were most of the time. They weren't the kind of true friends I have now.

In spite of the fact I had been saved and filled with the

Holy Spirit, I still felt lonely. The change in my life had dramatically improved my relationship with Donna, and we were enjoying sharing our new faith together.

Before long, however, my spiritual zeal started to get in the way. I wanted to go to every prayer meeting possible. We'd return home from one meeting and immediately be back in the car going to another. Some meetings were many miles away. We drove to Missouri, and over here and over there. We were getting fed spiritually but not in any one particular place.

Not only was it expensive traveling long distances, it was also affecting my work on the farm. Our finances were strained as a result of being constantly on the go.

At the same time, I had a compulsion to get rid of anything I enjoyed. I don't feel that way now, but I think it was valid at the time. One of the first things to go was my pool table. Since I associated it with drinking, bars, and partying, I sold the pool table. To this day I miss it.

The only friends I had were in the church, but I didn't want to talk about the Bible every second of every day. I wanted to talk about hunting and fishing.

I let the Bible dominate at first, but then I felt God was trying to control me and make me His slave. So I stopped being so consumed with God's Word. In the beginning, I just didn't understand the ways of God.

One day I had planned to go to Bill's house, but I told Donna, "I feel like going and getting drunk. I don't want to get drunk. I just want somebody to be my friend. I've got to have friends."

That night Donna and I prayed, "God, send us Christian friends." I had already planned to get drunk the next day, but three different families came by to visit. We had met them at the churches we'd been visiting. God answered our prayer, and we made new friends.

Before I knew God, I had tried to get into the Masons, but they wouldn't accept anyone who was a drunk. After I was saved and my life changed, they sent a representative to the house to check me out. He was impressed because all I wanted to talk about was Jesus.

"We'd like to have you join," I was told, "but we'd have to get a special waiver because of your hook." Apparently, I wouldn't be able to give the certain right-hand handshake.

I had a strong check in my spirit about becoming a Mason, but my pride over-rode my feelings because I'd wanted to join for so long. Now that I could, I felt I shouldn't.

I asked a Baptist preacher, "What does the Bible mean when it says you should not take an oath?"

"All that means is, if you take the oath, you are supposed to keep it." Then he added, "I'm a Mason."

So I joined the Masons. After attending one meeting and going through the ritual only once, I realized what they were doing didn't have anything to do with Jesus. In fact, I discovered that the organization was full of drunks. Yet, they had rejected me for years because I wasn't good enough.

When it came time for me to move up to the next level, a couple of fellow Masons offered to teach me the next ritual.

"You guys don't have to go to all that trouble," I said. I didn't know how to tell them that I didn't want to be a Mason after I'd become one. Finally I said, "Listen, I have a check in my spirit, and I don't want to go through any more of the training."

I didn't see a whole lot of sin there, but I didn't see anything of Jesus either. "Maybe this is all right for you guys, but it's more important for me to preach."

"This is like church," they said.

Well, of course, it wasn't like the churches that I was going to where we felt the presence of God.

Soon after Donna and I accepted Christ as our Saviour, we began taking in foster children and continued to do so for four years.

During this time we also had prayer meetings in our home on Sunday that generally lasted eight to ten hours.

Often they would continue late into the night. Sometimes the next morning 20 people would be sleeping on our living room floor. Those were really good times, and the people who came were godly Christians. Soon, however, an exclusive clique developed with the attitude: "We are the only ones. We have the answers."

They were encouraging me to preach, but I told them, "I'm not a preacher. I only wanted to work with foster kids." To make it emphatic, I said, "I will never preach!" I felt more like a Moses than an Aaron. I didn't feel qualified to preach.

When I'd been a drunk, you couldn't shut me up. But for the first few years after I was saved, I pretty much kept my mouth shut. In the meetings, they would ask, "Brother John, do you have a word from the Lord?"

I would answer, "No."

This went on for a long time.

Some time later, I was operating an earth mover for my neighbor, and he was running a bulldozer. He said, "John, we are building a dam here, and the result will be a 25-acre lake. Just drop the dirt here."

I said, "I don't see what we are doing."

"You don't have to see what we are doing. Just drop the dirt where I tell you," he replied.

I kept picking up the dirt, six or seven yards at a time, and dropped it where he said. At lunch I remarked, "I still don't see what we are doing."

"John," he said, "It doesn't make any difference. Just keep dropping the dirt where I tell you."

By the afternoon of the next day, I was able to visualize the project in my mind. I said, "Wow, I see what we are doing. I can see the dam taking shape."

That week while reading the Scriptures, I read in Isaiah 28:10, "Precept upon precept; line upon line; here a little, and there a little."

Because of my experience in building the dam, that verse became real to me.

Later that week at the prayer meeting, I was again asked, "Brother John, do you have something to share?"

I shared about the dam and the verse of Scripture that had become real to me. The people were blessed.

After that they couldn't shut me up. God began to stir something in me, and I had no choice but to share.

Previously, I thought I had to have a high school education, a college degree, Bible school, and seminary training before I could speak about spiritual things. Now I realized that as I studied the Word, God put in my heart teachings to share.

Before long, I was preaching in churches of every denomination. I even pastored one for a while called Miracle Temple.

I grew in the Lord. The prayer meetings continued, and our exclusiveness became more prevalent. One day I told the group, "I'd like to have my Baptist friends come to our meeting."

"Brother John, they wouldn't understand," they said. "Those people really haven't been called to this deep walk. You better just. . . ."

I backed off, but something happened in my heart, and I knew we were in error.

⌇⌇

Dale, a young evangelist whom I respected and had heard preach several times, was traveling in and out of Mexico building churches. Donna and I had been supporting his work. "I really want to make a trip with Dale," I told Donna.

Eventually, I saved up enough money to go. It was then I understood the Scripture, "For where your treasure is, there will your heart be also" (Luke 12:34).

We had been investing in Mexico for over a year. Before I left, one of the ladies in the prayer group prophesied over me, saying: "Thus saith the Lord thou shalt not go to Mexico. Surely curses will come unto thee and thy children if you go."

Because the prayer group was my only source of Christian fellowship, that "word" put real fear in my heart.

My spirit, however, kept urging me to go. I decided to listen to the Holy Spirit and follow God's leading.

I left Donna and the children in Arkansas on the farm and traveled with Dale to southern Mexico, almost to the Guatemalan border. We had a hassle with the Mexican police, and that scared me half to death.

I began to think, *I shouldn't have come. Maybe this trip is cursed.* Thank God, the prophecy wasn't true, and once in Mexico we were continually blessed.

Every place we stopped we drew a crowd, preached the gospel, sang, and handed out tracts. We even gave out candy to the children. When we arrived in the city of Huixtla, Mexico, we worked with a man named Ramon Mendosa. He cared for about 30 churches that he had founded. We went from church to church preaching the gospel and having a precious time in the Lord.

Some villagers would walk for 30 miles to attend church because they heard that Americans were going to share the gospel with them. At night we would see the people coming out of mountains with torches.

When they arrived, they were given a coffee bean sack as a mattress. Some nights there would be 150 people sleeping on the ground in front of the church on those sacks. The people stayed as long as we were there preaching — four days, three days, five days, or whatever. They wanted to hear about Jesus. I was deeply touched.

Some of our trips were hard on me physically. I spent a lot of time bouncing in the back of a pickup, but my heart was being forever changed. Now I had a tremendous burden to bring the message of Jesus Christ's salvation to the lost.

As far as the negative prophecy goes, as I continued to read and study the Scripture I found a jewel that says "Bless and curse not" (Rom. 12:14).

122

CHAPTER 12

Mexico

Donna, we are selling everything and moving to Mexico!'' I had just returned home from my trip and had no more gotten into the house when I blurted out the news.

Donna's father, a real saint, was there visiting us. Both he and Donna stood immobile as if they had been struck by lightning. "What do you mean?" she asked. "For the first time in eight years, we have a semblance of a home and family life. I'm not ready to give that up."

Donna and I made several trips back to Mexico, taking tons of donated clothing. Someone told us of a farmer who had bought discontinued shoes by the train loads to resell. Now he wanted to get out of the business. In a huge building that covered several acres, he had accumulated, over many years, thousands of shoes. They were scattered all over the building floor in piles about 20 inches high. "I was going to bulldoze them into a ditch," he told us, "but you can have them if you pick up the shoes and sort them."

We ended up with about 8,000 pairs that we took to Mexico and gave to several missions. That gift of new shoes made a lot of people happy.

<hr/>

We put our farm on the market, and it sold right away.

When the time came for us to leave for Mexico, we had to sell almost everything we owned. The house was basically furnished with all new furniture, dishes, and linens, but I was in such a hurry to leave that we almost gave everything away. We lost thousands of dollars.

I didn't give much thought to Donna's feelings. *After all,* I thought, *if she is spiritual, she will simply obey and follow me.* Believe it or not, that's exactly what she did! All we had left was our van and what it would hold.

At that time we had two children: Monique, 8, and John, 5. Four of us were living in that van. After driving to Mexico, we parked the van in the parking lot of a church. We stayed there for months, going out with the pastor from the church and ministering in the little villages.

The Mexican pastor and his wife had been given a wringer washing machine by some American missionaries and didn't know how to operate it. The pastor's wife still used a scrub board.

Donna tried the scrub board for a while until all of our clothes were full of holes. "I'm going to try to use the wringer washer," she told me one day. Since she had always used an automatic washing machine, Donna was not familiar with the wringer type.

Some American friends who wanted to see the work in Mexico were visiting with us at the time. "I was raised using a wringer washer," said the American lady. "Let's see if we can get it started." Soon they were washing our clothes in the old-fashioned machine.

"Let me help, Mommy," Monique begged.

Donna was a little leery but said, "Okay, but as you put these clothes through the wringer, you have to be very, very careful that you don't catch your hand."

Donna was hanging up some clothes on the line when suddenly she heard Monique screaming, "Mommy, Mommy, help me, help me!"

Donna turned around and saw Monique's little hand going through the wringer. Her thumb was pulled all the way back to her wrist where it was going backwards. At this point

Donna didn't know what to do and stood there in shock.

Suddenly, it was as if the Lord was saying, "Unplug the machine." She unplugged the machine, and the wringer stopped, but Monique's hand was still in it. Donna tried to pry it loose, but the wringer was as tight as it could be.

"John! Help us!" Donna began screaming. I was on the other side of the church sitting in our van talking with the man from America. I heard the screaming but thought it was some Mexicans going down the street chanting, so I didn't respond. Suddenly Donna came running around the church screaming, "Monique! Monique's hand, help!"

By the time I got there, her little hand was turning a purplish black. I started praying in the Spirit at the top of my lungs.

Donna was holding Monique, who was about to faint. I tried to get the roller apart, but the machine didn't have a quick release. I had to get a wrench to take the bolts apart. After loosening the bolts, I jammed my hook into the rollers and wedged it open enough to get Monique's hand out. Her hand was mangled and black.

As I had run around the church building to help Donna, I had started praying real loud. A group of Mexicans who had been standing across the street at another house ran over to see what was happening. About 20 of them were standing around me as I had worked to release Monique's hand.

Without thinking about it, I took her little hand and commanded it to be made whole in the name of Jesus. Then, in front of everybody, God did a miracle. Her little hand was completely restored. There wasn't even a red spot on it. I picked her up and held her for about a half-hour while she sobbed.

"Open and close your hand," I told her.

"No!" the American lady exclaimed. "That's the worst thing she can do!"

Monique opened and closed her hand. The Lord had healed her.

Living in the cramped van had become impossible. We were all unhappy, so I decided to purchase a 30-foot trailer.

This time we went to Laredo, Texas, to work with Herb Bargo and several missions he had there. We were living in a veterinarian's back yard just inside Texas. Since it was summer, the temperature in our living room would climb to 130 degrees. Our two box fans didn't help much.

We had several big air-conditioners under the rented mobile home, but we didn't have the money to turn them on because we were using our money for Mexico. I was going across the border 2 or 3 times a day preaching.

On one such a trip I met a lady who asked me to speak at her church that night. When I arrived, there was no interpreter. The pastor only knew two words of English and said, "You preach."

I said, "But I don't speak Spanish."

The pastor again said, "You preach."

I preached in the Spirit. I used a couple of words in Latin I had learned as a child in the Catholic church and also preached in English. I acted out everything as best I could with a lot of prayer.

As a result, 17 people gave their hearts to the Lord that night. Several people were even healed.

Soon we were asked to pastor a Mexican church.

"I don't speak Spanish," I told them.

"That okay," they said.

"Where is the church?" I asked.

"In that little blue house," they showed me. "We are renting it." I became the pastor.

Some people who didn't want a new church in that area would throw rocks and break the windows of the house. The owner of the property said he could not rent it to be used as a church any longer.

A Mexican lady named Sister Johnson and her husband who owned a trucking company donated a small plot of land. Our little church started out with three women and some kids. I drove stakes in the ground and nailed two-by-fours on top of them for people to sit on. That was our church. No roof, no sides, nothing. Since we preached under a mesquite tree where the chickens roosted, I jokingly told the people, "You have to be a little pentecostal." Whenever something dropped out of the tree, the people had to move in a big hurry!

As the congregation grew, Herb Bargo helped us build a new building in a period of ten months. Soon we had over 100 people, with many giving their hearts to the Lord.

During this time, I was also ministering in Laloma prison. Although it was dangerous to preach in Mexico's prisons, the Lord led me to take the gospel to the desperate inmates incarcerated there.

As I was escorted through the many gates, the guards would stick their machine guns in my face and push me through each one. I went to the prison three times a week, ministering to a lot of Americans who were there on drug charges. Many of them were innocent, but everybody in a Mexican jail is guilty because they have signed a confession.

I talked to one man who showed me his feet where they had taken pliers and pulled all of his toe nails out to get him to sign the confession. I talked to other men who had an electric cattle prod used on them. They tied their hands and feet, stripped them of their clothes, threw a bucket of water on them, and followed them around like a worm on the floor with an electric cattle prod until they would sign the confession.

One day, I talked to a man who was fine. The next day I went back and saw a bone sticking out of his wrist because one guard had held his wrist while another guard took a stick and broke it.

It wasn't a very nice place. When there was a knife fight going on between the prisoners, the guards would bet on who was going to win. Then they would stand back and watch what happened.

In spite of the circumstances, I made a lot of friends there and preached the gospel to the inmates. Many Mexican and American men came to Christ. I also had the blessing of leading 21 Salvadorian men to the Lord. They had been picked up by the Mexican government while trying to escape the fighting in El Salvador. To say the least, it was an interesting place.

One day a Mexican lawyer came to me and said, "Don't go back into the prison anymore."

"Why not?" I asked.

"Because they were going to throw you in a cell and keep you there," he told me.

"But I haven't done anything wrong."

"John, all they have to do is plant marijuana on you and say that you were bringing it in to the prisoners."

"Why would they do that?" I asked.

"To extort money from your family," he explained.

When the lawyer told me that, I prayed and fasted because I wanted to go back into the prison. By then I had been visiting there for ten months and wanted a chance to say goodbye to the men.

The lawyer again said, "If you go back, they will keep you. I am telling you the truth. I am not a Christian, but I respect you and what you are doing. Don't go back."

The Holy Spirit led me to the Scripture that said, "But when they persecute you in this city, flee ye into another" (Matt. 10:23).

Donna and I sat outside the prison at Laloma, and I cried because I didn't want to leave my friends. But there wasn't anything else I could do. My family couldn't do much good in Mexico without a husband and father.

⌐▮⌐

On that trip we were in Mexico a year working every day. Most of our ministry was financed out of my disability pension.

While we were building the church, a man came to watch and I was allowed to lead him to the Lord. After that, he came every day on his bicycle to help.

He was about 60 years old and cleaned yards for a couple of dollars a day. When we were taking up collections to build the church, he came with about $60 in coins in a bag and gave it to me. That was about two months' wages. It really touched my heart.

"Pastor John," he said, "My Catholic father, who is in his eighties, wants to be led to the Lord. Will you come and minister to him?"

I said, "Sure." He gave me the address. The next day I drove all over town and finally found the house on a corner lot. Open on two sides, the tiny one- room house consisted of a roof only partly covered with a couple of pieces of tin.

Their beds were two wide planks at 90 degree angles. The dad slept on one and Ramon slept on the other. There was a fire in the middle of the room. It humbled me to realize that this man gave the church $60.

I prayed with Ramon's father, and he received the Lord that day. A short time later, both Ramon and his father died. I know they have a mansion in heaven.

An 80-year-old woman named Lopeta came to church and was saved. Although it was winter, she insisted on being baptized right away. "I don't want to wait," she told me.

In Mexico it is against the law for an American to perform a sacrament. I decided to baptize her in the Rio Grande River since it was on the American border. The water was very cold, but that didn't bother her one bit.

Lopeta lived in a one-room shack with big cracks in all the walls. "You must be cold in the winter," I told her.

We bought some tar paper and hired a man to staple it over the cracks so she could stay warm.

When the church was finished, my friend, Teto Ibarra, dedicated the building. As a teenager, Teto had been para-lyzed from the neck down when he hit his head after diving into a flooded garbage dump.

When I first went to minister to Teto, he was 21 years old and already a Christian. He lived with his mother in a little room — perhaps only eight by nine feet — that was cold in the winter and hot in the summer.

Teto did not have an easy life. His mother was very bitter and hateful because she had to take care of him. His body was rigid and straight, stretched out in his wheelchair.

We carried him to church in the back of a pickup truck.

During most of the dedication service all I could do was weep. As Teto spoke, the anointing of God flowed out to everyone there. As I looked out at the people, I thought, *God, these people have no idea the depths of sin that I have been involved in, yet they look up to me.*

Even though I was serving the Lord, I still had a lot of flashbacks about Vietnam. I had quit drinking, quit taking drugs, and the hatred and bitterness were gone from my life. All that mattered to me now was ministering to those in need and seeing lives changed by the power of Jesus Christ.

Altogether we spent about six years in and out of Mexico. Many good things happened.

CHAPTER 13

Uncharted Waters

In 1979, I traveled to Belize for the first time. I accompanied Brother Holly and one of his friends who were of the Oneness persuasion. We drove an old van with the intention of selling it because vehicles are worth more money in Belize. If we sold it, we would have enough money to fly back.

During the entire trip, Brother Holly and Brother Jimmy — who are dear friends and will be until we die — were trying to convince me to be baptized in Jesus' name only. They quoted to me Acts 10:48 and 19:5: "Be baptized in Jesus' name. . . ."

I quoted back to them Matthew 28:19: "In the name of the Father, and of the Son, and of the Holy Ghost." I tried to expound on the fact that the word "name" in Greek says honor, authority, and character. In other words, it is the nature of God that we are baptized into. Baptism is an act of obedience to God, and we are baptized unto Him. We battled back and forth, back and forth and went round and round. They were adamant on this subject.

When we arrived at the Caribbean Sea, I said, "Baptize me."

"Praise God. You got the revelation!" they exclaimed.

"No," I answered, "the Lord and me are fine, but if I am a stumbling block to you, I don't want to be. I want you to baptize me in Jesus' name, and that will take care of your problem." They wouldn't baptize me. During our trip, I did most of the preaching and they did all the baptizing.

᚛‖᚜

As we traveled across Mexico, we held revival meetings. For a couple hundred miles we followed a dirt road to Punta Gorda at the southern tip of Belize, next to Honduras. As we approached the village, the road was full of deep, muddy potholes. We probably passed 50 vehicles stuck in the mud in various places.

The local people, knowing we were on a mission for God, blessed us with tires for our vehicle. That was a precious gift because our tires were really taking a beating. Brother Holly had spent several years working with these people so they knew him.

We had just arrived when a village lady came to us carrying her week-old baby. Weighing only four pounds, the baby had a fiery red boil about the size of a golf ball in the center of her chest. "My baby will die without medicine," she told us.

"Why is the baby dressed in a christening gown?" I asked Brother Holly.

"The mother has given up hope and has prepared the child for burial," he replied.

Our hearts were so touched that we travailed in prayer for the baby. After prayer, we went on about our business. The next day, the boil broke, and the baby began nursing. Wherever we went in the village, when the mother saw us, she raised her hands and proclaimed, "Praise the Lord! Praise the Lord! My baby is healed!"

᚛‖᚜

Belize is a beautiful country with an interesting mix of cultures. English is spoken, plus the various native tongues of the Carob Africans, Indians from East India, Kikche Indians, Miya Indians, and the Spanish people.

In the afternoon, we might visit people from East India

WOUNDED SOLDIER

132

who lived in huts with cow dung floors, and our meal was rice and curry. In the evening, we could be eating a meal of gibnut, which is like a big rat they catch in the jungle, with Carob Africans.

One day, a man named Gabriel asked, "Do you want to go tiger hunting?

"How do we do that?" I inquired.

He showed me a lid from a tin can that he had put two holes in and folded. "Brother John, when we blow into this, it makes a squealing sound like a wounded rabbit's scream. At night we find a tiger trail and put dry leaves on the trail. Then we sit in the bushes about six or seven feet from the trail with a flashlight and our gun (which was a 16-gauge, single shot). We blow the whistle and when the tiger comes, we turn on our flashlight and shoot the tiger," he explained.

"What do you do if you don't kill the tiger?" I asked.

His eyes got big. Then he reached by his belt and said, "Ah, the machete."

"I would really like to go tiger hunting with you, but I'm afraid I'm not going to have any free nights while I'm here ministering," I said, excusing myself.

While we were ministering to a Kikche Indian tribe, we stayed in a small house that Brother Holly had built years before. These little black flies could go right through the window screens at 90 miles an hour — and did they bite. To keep from being eaten alive, we kept smoking insecticide snakes by our bed.

One night there was a knock on the door. When we opened the door, there stood the son of a Kikche Indian chief. "Come in," we invited.

"God told me to build a church in the middle of the jungle, and I have obeyed Him," he said. "And I want you to come and dedicate the church. My people need to know about Jesus Christ."

It was like something out of the Book of Acts. We felt God was leading us to go with him. The next morning, we got into a 20-foot-long, hollowed-out log with a 20-horsepower Johnson motor on the back. We motored up the Caribbean

Sea for several hours and then turned up the Monkey River and traveled for another hour. The river was so clear we could see beautiful multi-colored fish dashing in and out of the rocks.

Although the scenery was awesome and beautiful, the bugs were terrible. Iguana lizards and hundreds of monkeys moved about high up in the overhanging trees. Occasionally we saw a tiger.

As lunch time approached, our hosts decided it would be nice to have a female iguana for lunch. "They aren't as strong tasting as the male," he explained.

We looked and looked, but didn't find any. As we got closer to the village, I noticed we were passing a lot of male lizards. "Let me kill one of the males," I suggested.

I spotted one about six feet long on the top of a tree. When I shot it, he came down with claws and head snapping. It splashed into the water next to us, and the guys maneuvering the canoe beat him to death with their paddles. He was our lunch.

The Indian had built a little bamboo church 12 x 20 feet. For an altar they had been put two stakes in the ground with a board across the top. When we arrived, the Indians sent out the village warriors in their canoes to bring in people for the church service. Some of the villagers had been to Catholic services in town before, but most had never attended an evangelical service where the gospel was preached. Soon the church was full.

We were in the middle of the jungle with only a river or a trail as an entrance. As we preached the Word, the Holy Spirit began touching people's lives. One after another, they began to repent and accept Christ as their Saviour.

What a wonderful experience. I will never forget it.

While up the river, I met an Australian man who had fought for Australia during the Vietnam war. He apparently couldn't cope and had moved to Belize where he escorted Europeans on tiger hunts. (What they call tigers are more like leopards or panthers.)

This man had three wives, a grass hut, a canoe, and

sophisticated weapons. He had isolated himself in his own world.

Although he was very cordial, I couldn't get close to him because he had built a protective "wall" around himself — like so many of us American vets had done.

I made several more trips to Central America. Every visit was enjoyable and brought me fulfillment as people's lives were changed for Christ. Nothing thrilled me more than seeing the power of the Holy Spirit working in these countries.

Working in uncharted waters — whether it be with Vietnam veterans or in some foreign country — where the people haven't been brainwashed with religiosity — is always more rewarding.

CHAPTER 14

Miracles in Haiti

After Belize, the Lord laid on my heart to make a trip to Haiti. At that time I was part of the ministry at "Jesus Is Lord Ministries" run by Charles Thompson.

When Charles and several of his team decided to go to Haiti, I went with them. Soon after our arrival, I hired a taxi cab and went off by myself. Wherever I saw sick and hurting people, I stopped to pray for them. I prayed for people on the street and on the steps of the Catholic church. I wouldn't do that now unless God led me that way again.

While in Haiti, my heart was touched by the people, and God placed a special burden on my heart for that destitute country.

In the evenings, Brother Charles held large crusades, and we saw many miracles. Four of us shared the ministry. After the altar call, each of us had several hundred people in a healing line wanting prayer. Several people in my line claimed that they had received their hearing back. I didn't know if they did or not, but I continued to pray.

Since I had contracted dysentery and was feeling miserable, I wasn't exercising very much faith during the service. All I wanted to do was get some Pepto Bismol, go to the hotel, and lie down.

Just then an old lady came up for prayer. She was bent over and had been crippled from birth.

I didn't have my prosthesis (arm) on that night. Usually I just touch a person on the head or hold his or her hand when I pray. For some reason, I put my stump and my hand on this old lady's waist. In my heart I wanted to say a quick prayer and get out of there. I felt sick.

As I began to pray for her, the anointing of God came on me. I can't explain it other than I felt bones breaking inside this woman. The noise was so loud that it scared me. She screamed and stood straight up. "I have never been able to run my entire life!" she told me. But that night she did — all over the tabernacle!

When people who knew her as the old crippled lady saw her standing straight, they too began to scream and shout. The place went wild with joy. Once again I was privileged to see a creative miracle of God. That increased my faith, and I was no longer concerned about my dysentery.

The need in Haiti is so great that it almost overwhelms anyone who tries to be of help. I am certain that most of the pastors in Haiti love the Lord and want the best for their people. Some, however, are in the "business" to fleece the American Christians. I met one such man. I'll call him Rev. Juan Doe.

Rev. Juan took me to an orphanage he was operating. In front of the dirty and run-down building was an ever-burning garbage dump where all of the locals brought their garbage. The stench, smoke, and fumes were beyond belief. "This is where the children must play," he told me.

It reminded me of what "hell" must be like. The children had sores all over their little bodies and most had head lice. That day, with tears streaming down my face, I made a commitment to God and to Rev. Juan, "I will do everything I can to help these children."

When I returned to the States, I started raising money. I took my family all around the United States, sleeping in the car. If I preached and raised $15, that $15 went to Haiti. I paid for all of my own expenses and never took a dime of the money I raised. Week after week, I continued to send money. Before long, I was sending thousands of dollars for the children at the orphanage. At one point, I brought Rev. Juan to the States so we could raise more money for "his" work.

On one of my trips to Haiti, Juan came to me saying, "Brother John, someone just brought this little girl to us. She was found in the jungle screaming while her mother lay dying. Would you like to adopt her?"

I went to the orphanage to look at her. It broke my heart every time I saw the hungry and neglected children there. When I walked over to little Maria's crib, she was screaming as loudly as she could. I looked down at her, and she held out her little hands wanting me to pick her up. At six months, she was only skin and bone, and her little belly was extended like a pot-belly stove. As I picked her up, she clung to me and squeezed me. She desperately wanted someone to love her.

I began making regular visits to Haiti and bought a car there so I could have my own transportation and travel where I wanted. I felt so sorry for Maria and the other children that I would do anything to help Rev. Juan. I wept, I cried, I begged, I borrowed. I flew him around the United States.

Then the shock came! I learned that Rev. Juan was with the TonTonmaque, the secret police in Haiti and carried a .38 pistol. The "members" of his church were forced to attend. A few of the orphans were really orphans, but most were neighbors' kids who were gathered up whenever the Americans got off the plane. Juan always had his spies at the airport.

I later discovered that many of the children living in Haitian orphanages actually have parents. The so-called "pastors," knowing they can get more money, purposely keep the children malnourished in a bogus orphanage. The bigger the orphanage, the more money the swindlers get from people in the States. It would be better to let the children stay at home and give the parents the money for food.

When I discovered the truth, anger, disappointment, and hurt welled up inside me all at the same time. I also learned that he had two orphanages, and depending on which Americans got off the plane, he moved the children from building to building. One group was supporting this building, and the other was supporting the other building.

His workers told me in confidence, "We were ordered to keep the children with swelled bellies and red hair because if the children weren't starving, the Americans wouldn't give much money."

The donations that I gave him went into property that he purchased for himself around the city. While I had my family sleeping in the back of an old car raising money, he was buying $35 shirts.

I felt really stupid.

"You're nothing but a liar and a cheat who uses the suffering of innocent children to line your own pockets!" I shouted at Juan when I confronted him.

He didn't deny anything.

"I know you have a gun!" I declared boldly. "Why don't you use it!" I was at the point of killing him — I was so angry.

Juan started hollering, "You have to forgive me. The Bible says you have to forgive me."

I shouted back, "The Bible says 'bring forth therefore fruits meet for repentance.' Juan, I will personally escort you to the edge of hell and push you in."

"You have to forgive me! You have to forgive me!" he kept shouting.

I got right in his face and shouted, "If you don't shut up, they're going to carry you out of here feet first!"

"Brother, you can't do that!" he exclaimed.

"I could do that if God would let me. You can thank God that I'm not God."

He said, "But you can't tell anybody what I have done. It will make you look stupid to your friends, and it will hurt your ministry."

I answered, "Brother, I have to be a person of integrity and honor, and when I get home, I will tell everyone about you."

Then I went to the workers and asked about little Maria. Apparently, she was used as a come-on for American suckers.

"Her mother is alive and paid for the use of her starving

baby," we were told. Donna and I were heartbroken over that precious infant.

One of the hardest things I have ever had to do was write a letter explaining that I had been deceived by Rev. Juan and apologizing for bringing him to their churches. That letter stopped most of our financial support. That was okay. I had to tell the truth. Some Christians told me, "You should just let it die and not say anything."

"I can't do that," I said. "This kind of corruption demands that the lies be exposed — no matter what it costs me personally."

When I returned home, I was bitter, upset, and disillusioned — not just by the pastors and missionaries I had met in Haiti, but by several other Christian people I had held in high esteem. Since I was a only a young Christian, this experience was very painful. That is why it is so important for us to keep our eyes on the Lord and not on a person.

Although the Haiti incident was a devastating setback, I knew there was still a bona fide need there. Now I was educated and knew how to work with people. From that point on, when I went back to Haiti, I worked closely with the local people and governed how every dime was spent.

᙭ᔋᔕ

When Donna was about eight months pregnant, I said to her, "As soon as you have the baby, I want to go back to Haiti. And I feel like the Lord wants you and the children to go with me." Donna and the children had never been to Haiti with me.

"John, you're crazy. Haiti is full of disease and horrible things like voodoo and spiritualism," she informed me. "I'm not going and neither are the children — let alone a brand-new baby."

About a month later, our second son, David, was born and had what the doctor called "failure to thrive." That was a fancy name he used to tell us that David was dying. Small and weighing only six pounds when he was born, he continued to lose weight.

"I can't go to Haiti with our sick baby," Donna told me.

I didn't question her, but said, "I'm going to let the Lord speak to your heart, and when you're ready, then we'll go."

The baby continued to lose weight and looked horrible. When David's weight dropped below four pounds, all of our friends agreed with Donna that we shouldn't go — or we would have a baby buried in Haiti.

Then Donna came to me and said, "John, the baby is going to die anyway, and I really believe that we should all be together." So we went to Haiti as a family.

In that obedience to the Lord, He blessed us, and David began to eat and eat. He put on weight immediately; his color changed, and in two weeks he became a very healthy baby. God performed a miracle!

~ ❦ ~

On this trip to Haiti, I had more wisdom under my belt. I was more cautious and — I suppose — more cynical. I still wanted to see people saved and lives changed, but I didn't trust anybody. I made every person I had dealings with prove everything to me.

We stayed in the north part of Carfu, a slummy suburb of Port-au-Prince. We planned on staying six weeks.

A girl had come along with us to help Donna, and we were all planning to stay in a small orphanage. "We can't stay here!" Donna exclaimed. "This place is filthy!"

For days we worked disinfecting the entire building and getting the toilet to work. Then we painted everything in sight. The seven of us lived in two small rooms separated by a sheet. From there we went out every day to work with the children and evangelize the neighborhoods.

The Lord had laid on my heart the need to start a work in San Luis, which was about 150 miles away. We purchased a house that a pastor had been renting for an orphanage and spent a week painting and disinfecting it, too. Our goal was to prepare the house so the kids could live in it safely.

As we were returning from working on the orphanage in San Luis and heading back toward Port-au-Prince, we were stopped at a roadblock. The police — who are really the military — had nearly 20 miles of traffic stopped dead. "What's going on?" we asked someone.

"Some rebels parachuted in, killed about 17 Haitian soldiers, and took their uniforms." They called this incident "the invasion of Tortuga."

The Haitian soldiers who stopped us were scared to death. "Americans!" they shouted back and forth. Apparently, 23 of the paratroopers were Americans. "What are you doing on this part of the island?" they asked us. Tourists didn't usually come to that section of Haiti.

As we waited in the hot, steamy car, we watched as the soldiers took some people into buildings. They slapped them around and beat them up, trying to get information out of them.

When they got to us, they waved their rifles around our heads and faces. Then they checked the car. "Open the glove box!" they demanded.

I didn't know how to open it since I had borrowed the vehicle from a pastor. I began praying, "Oh, God, I pray there isn't a gun in that glove box because if there is, we are all dead." They were about to take their weapon and beat the box open when I finally found the key to open it. There wasn't anything in there, thank God.

One of the soldiers grabbed the purse of the interpreter who had accompanied us. I had just given her $200 to help with her work in Haiti. He took the money out and put it into his pocket.

They tried to intimidate us, and it worked. We were kept there for eight hours. It was extremely hot, and my kids were getting sick from dehydration.

One of the soldiers began waving his rifle in my face and hollering at me in broken English.

"I don't understand!" I kept telling him. "I don't speak Creole!" Finally I got real upset and drove out of the line to the other lane. Since no cars were coming from the other direction, there was plenty of room to drive.

When we arrived at the next road block, I started

yelling, "Get out of the way and let us through!" I didn't know if we would be shot or what would happen. To my surprise, we got through and continued on to Port-au-Prince.

Praise God. That was another miracle.

❧

When we got back to the orphanage, we were met in the hallway by rats as big as most house cats. That was nothing compared to the evil that awaited us.

During our open-air services in the evenings when we were worshiping the Lord, a demon-possessed girl would sometimes start writhing on the ground and screaming, "Can't you see they are trying to pull me into the ground?" When she went into these screaming fits, her eyes would glaze over and her face took on a crazed expression. Someone told us that this girl had tried to drown a little orphan baby.

On three separate occasions, we prayed for her and ministered deliverance from the evil forces that controlled her. When we left the island, she was doing very well, had returned to school, and was in her right mind.

This part of Carfu was a good place to go crazy. Voodoo witch doctors lived nearby in houses on both sides of us. Most of the time we would go to bed at 10:30 or 11:00. We would just get to sleep when we could hear the screams begin and see the fires light up. The drum beats alone were enough to drive us mad since they were only 10 or 12 feet away. Although the orphanage where we lived had no windows — only cement blocks turned on end for air to pass through — we were bombarded by the sounds of their heathen rituals.

Even during the day they would put on a show for us. The witch doctor would gather up 75 or more people in front of the orphanage, and they would beat drums, scream, and try to scare us. Our family would stand on the front porch of the orphanage, praying. We knew our God was greater than any hex or "demon" they could produce. As they did this, we never made any violent moves toward them. Soon they gave up and moved on.

Some of the men were naked except for a loin cloth and white stripes painted on their black bodies. Each man had a rope tied around his neck and would run around on all fours like an animal.

By the time we were ready to return to the States, Donna and the children had accumulated plenty of stories to tell the folks back home.

We felt we had done good work in the slums and seen a lot of Haitian people come to Christ.

───

When we returned to the States, everyone was amazed when they saw "big" David. In six weeks, he had gained 13 pounds and hasn't been sick since.

Before long, I returned to Haiti for a short trip to visit the orphanage. At that time there were 16 orphans, the pastor, and his family living in one large room. My goal was to add a room onto the orphanage for the pastor and his wife — an 8 x 20 foot addition. Several Haitians were going to help me.

"Look, guys, I have four days to build this room on the side of the orphanage," I told them.

"Brother John, it'll take a couple of months," they said. "Just leave the money, and we will take care of building the room."

By this time, I wasn't leaving money anywhere unless I could see what it was doing. "All the material that I have purchased will be returned to the supplier when I leave," I said, making my intentions clear. "What we do in the next four days is what you will have. So I suggest we get to work, and now. If you really want a room, we can build it."

I hired several unemployed people from the church and paid them the customary wages of $2 a day. Some of them wanted more money, but I didn't give in to their demands. We worked day and night, but some workers would stand around doing nothing. At times I got physical and shook them to make them go to work.

One night I was working on finishing the concrete floor. I am not a finisher, but I was out there doing my best, trying to smooth off the floor about 10:00 at night. Since San Luis had no electricity at the time, I was working by the light of a Coleman lantern.

This was the season of the Mardi Gras and — according to Haitian tradition — the night that voodoo priests can fly.

Suddenly, I heard a racket coming down the street: drums beating and people screaming. Then I saw a crowd of people who were gyrating and acting crazy.

I thought, *Surely they will continue down the main street. Most likely they don't want anything to do with me.*

To my surprise, about 500 people came right down the alley and stopped where I was working. I walked up onto a pile of sand so I was standing a little higher than the crowd. They moved around and completely surrounded me.

These guys are so skinny, I could probably take out any 10 of them, I said to myself.

As they tried to frighten and intimidate me, the Lord gave me complete peace. I didn't know what was going on, but I figured it wasn't any good. They pointed their torches at me and continued shouting, chanting, and jumping up and down.

I just stood there and prayed in the Spirit.

The five witch doctors were grouped together. God gave me the gift of fearlessness, and I looked right through them. When they realized I wasn't afraid, the chanting stopped and they all turned around and left.

I hadn't noticed, but as soon as the crowd had approached, all my co-workers had taken off. When the people left, they all came back out.

"What was happening here? What were they saying?" I asked.

They answered, "They were chanting, 'What should we do with the one-armed white man? What should we do with the one-armed white man?' "

Different ones would holler out different things like, "We should kill him."

Then they started chanting again: "Leave him alone. He is a good one-armed white man. He helps the Haitians."

In many Third World countries, a man is looked down on as handicapped if he has an arm, an eye, or a leg missing. I thank God that He gave me the respect of the people.

Here I was working with some perfectly healthy — but basically lazy — men, and I could outwork any of them with one hand. They realized I wasn't in Haiti to take pictures and go back home to raise money. They knew I wasn't there to exalt myself. I was there because the Lord laid on my heart to add a room on for their pastor and his wife.

I knew I had earned their respect.

When we finished, the workers made a sign with my name and the name of my ministry on it. Then they placed it in front of the orphanage.

I knew from past experience that the Haitians knew how to work on a man's ego and pride, so I said to the pastor, "If this were my orphanage, the children would be cleaner than they are and so would the building. This is not my orphanage. You are the one who has the responsibility to keep it going. Take my name down."

CHAPTER 15

Vietnam —
Curse or Blessing?

"John, you should write a book," people would often say to me. I thought, *You have to be kidding. I only have a ninth grade education.* (I later got my GED.)

Over the years, I had shared my testimony about Vietnam a few times and told how the Lord had set me free and spared my life. Although it was painful for me, I wanted to reach vets who were suffering.

When wives of Vietnam vets heard my testimony, they would come up to me and say, "John, that really helped me to understand my husband." Some people gave their hearts to the Lord after hearing my testimony. I even had two authors call the house asking if they could work with me on a book. I said, "No."

Then I began to think about it. After about a year or two, I decided maybe I should do a book.

Some friends of ours in Batesville, Arkansas, heard Cliff Dudley (author of *Like A Mighty Wind*) speak. I gave him a call, and he agreed to write my book.

I had no idea what I was getting into when Cliff and I began working together. Using a tape recorder, he would ask me questions, and I would answer them. I wanted to skip over the painful parts, but Cliff would ask me how I felt, what it smelled like, what guys said before they died.

While working on the book, I would sometimes flip out, cuss, and run upstairs. At other times, Cliff would hold me like a little boy and pray for me.

As I look back, I realize that the painful and traumatic experience of writing a book was actually a time of deliverance for me. It taught me a lot about working with other veterans and how to counsel and minister to them. A person can be a Christian, even Spirit-filled, and still have a lot of scars and hurts from the past that haven't healed.

After Cliff completed the taping, it was up to him to put it all down on paper. I tried again to forget Nam.

⇜❧⇝

When the book *Vietnam, Curse or Blessing?* first came out, I was scared to death. By then we had moved to Moberly, Missouri. When the congregation of Lighthouse Christian Ministries asked me to be their pastor, I said I would until they could get someone else. The church also had a Christian school, and I served as its principal for three years.

In the meantime, the book came out.

Since I had gone through so much agony writing my past experiences, I didn't want to think about the book. The last thing I need, I told myself, is to be constantly reminded of all my painful memories. I was like a woman who, after writing a cookbook, stated she wasn't going to cook anymore! That is how I felt. I was trying to take Vietnam out of my life and make it disappear. But I couldn't.

No matter what our experiences in life, the Scripture says ". . . all things work together for good to them that love God, to them who are called according to His purpose" (Rom. 8:28).

While I was trying to run from the book, I wrote to Mark Buntain (a missionary to India) that my wife, children, and I had about eight years of missionary service in various countries and would like to come work with him in Calcutta, India. I even sent him a check for $100.

Mark never received the letter, and the check was never

cashed. Apparently, God had other plans.

After the book was published, I began receiving calls from people asking me questions about Vietnam veterans.

When I had told my story to Cliff, I thought I was the only veteran who was dealing with the effects of my Vietnam experience. I was uninformed about the unique problems other veterans were going through. Since then I have learned there are tens of thousands of Vietnam vets who have gone through the same struggles. My first book, *Vietnam, Curse or Blessing?* has become almost a standard text for use in some therapy and support groups. I had no idea that God would use my story to touch the lives of so many other veterans.

"We have a group of vets in prison. I wonder if you would like to come out and speak to them?" The voice on the other end of the phone was J.C. Right of the Missouri Training Center for Men — a medium and partially maximum security prison in Moberly. As a Vietnam veteran and a psychologist, J.C. was working with a Vietnam veterans' support group.

"How many vets do you have in your prison?" I asked.

"We have 1,600 inmates, and 200 of them are Vietnam veterans," he replied.

"Two hundred!" I exclaimed. "You're kidding."

"I wish I were," J.C. said. "In fact, there are 71,000 vets incarcerated in the United States." That fact blew me away.

"I really enjoyed reading your book," he told me, "but I'm not too sure about the God part in the back of it."

I had long ago told the Lord that I would go anyplace and do anything for Him, so I said, "Yes, J.C., I'll come."

After I said yes, I realized I would be looking eyeball to eyeball with numerous Vietnam veterans. Then I thought, *They're coming to hear me tell how I got my act together.* I was scared to death and didn't want to do it, but I had said I would. I went to the prison with only one message in my heart: "Jesus loves me, this I know, for the Bible tells me so."

I had already decided I was going to dump it on these guys and run.

After I got through the second set of electric gates at the prison, a group of Vietnam vets met me before we went upstairs. They hugged me, and for the first time ever, I heard, "Welcome home, John. Thank you for fighting for our country." Nobody had ever thanked me for fighting in Vietnam. I could hardly handle all of my emotions. I thought I would pass out.

We went upstairs to the "rap" group, and the four-letter words started bouncing off the walls. My religious spirit got offended, and I said to God, "Listen to this filthy language."

The Lord spoke to my heart and said, "They sound just like you used to — and still do when you slam your finger in a car door." That kicked the religious props out from under me.

Before I left, they asked me if I would be their chaplain. "You have got to be kidding," I replied. "What are you people, anyway?"

That day I had met black Moslems, a Buddhist, a Jehovah's Witness, a Christian Scientist, and even a few Christians. There was a little bit of everything.

"Guys, I don't care if you sprinkle, dunk, or pour, but Jesus Christ is more than a good man, more than a good prophet," I told them frankly. "He is the only name under heaven whereby men can be saved. He is the Son of God. If you confess with your mouth and believe with your heart in the Lord Jesus, you will be saved."

I thought my reply would change their minds. Instead, they said, "Brother John, we'll forgive you for believing that. We want you anyway."

Even if they didn't agree with my beliefs in Christianity, these men were still willing to accept me — no questions asked. Unfortunately, I wanted to accept them only if they would let me put them in my box and make them believe exactly how I wanted them to believe. They wanted me to be their chaplain anyway, and I accepted.

I became the chaplain of the Incarcerate of Vietnam

Veterans Organization — the first one, as far as I know. It was Vietnam Veterans of America Chapter 70 of Moberly, Missouri, and we had about 40 in the group. During the next three years, I had the privilege of leading many of those men to Christ.

Upon their release from prison, several of the inmates from that group have come to see me, and I have established quite a friendship with them. My experience as a prison chaplain thrust me into the ministry for which God had been preparing me for many years — working with, what I consider to be the finest people in America, veterans.

⛬

At the session of the Incarcerate of Vietnam Veterans Organization, the inmates said, "Reverend John Steer, would you like to open with prayer?" It seemed ironic to open a rap session with prayer when four-letter words were flying around with almost every breath. I invited the Lord to be present with us — especially since I, for one, wanted Him to be there!

"Reverend? What in the h— is a reverend doing in here?" one inmate wanted to know. I later learned he had served during the Korean War and was a black Era veteran. "I thought this group was for combat veterans!" he sneered.

"Look, man!" I said, getting right up in his face.. "You've got no right to insult me!" Although he was a large man, I started to get physical.

"Back off!" the other guys told him. "This reverend was in Vietnam and saw more combat than you have in your dreams!" As it turned out, he was the only one who wasn't a combat veteran. The only "combat" he had known was shooting and killing witnesses — like old men and women — who had seen him rob Seven-11 stores. In fact, he had been nicknamed the "Seven-11 killer"

The next time I visited the prison, this man came up to me and apologized. He said, "Rev. John, I'll never make that mistake again."

When a riot occurred in the prison and made national headlines, some of the men wanted me to exploit it. "You can talk about this problem on your radio show," they suggested.

"I can't do that because I wasn't an eyewitness to what happened," I explained. "I would only be spreading hearsay." I had been told that if I said anything about the problem in the prison on the air, I would never be allowed to visit another prison. I shared that with the men and asked them, "Do you want me to come back or not?"

"You're just chicken!" one man shouted angrily.

The rest of the men jumped on him. "Shut up, or we're gonna kill you!" they threatened.

All I had to do was nod my head, and they would have torn his head off. I said, "No, that's not the way to solve this."

One of the prison supervisors called me into his office and said, "You're the same as a paid employee here and have no business breathing a word of what goes on here to the outside." I remained silent about the way the guards handled the riot.

During this time, I also started a Sunday morning service at the prison called "Soldiers for Christ." Before long, 30 to 40 Vietnam vets were coming to church on Sunday.

I wasn't into the "repeat-after-me" conversion method. I would rather have someone come to me and tell me he has had an experience with the Lord than have him repeat a "my words" prayer. Nor did I pat the guys on the back and tell them to be good boys. I simply preached the gospel.

"If something has happened in your life," I told them, "if you are praying — or if you have repented and asked Christ to forgive you for your sins — you will know you are saved. Nobody will have to tell you."

As the men began to tell me their stories about their experiences in Vietnam, the taste and smell of burning flesh accumulated in the back of my throat making me nauseated. I didn't want to hear any war stories because they brought back bad memories. The Lord reminded me, however, that the Scripture tells us not only to "rejoice with them that do rejoice," but also to "weep with them that weep" (Rom. 12:15).

The only way we can understand someone's pain is to have been through the same experience ourselves. (Of course, the Holy Spirit can give us sympathy for someone.)

The Lord spoke to my heart, saying that it was time for me to start working with veterans, whether I felt like it or not.

All people are experts at something. If they are Christians and have made it through a crisis in their lives, they are experts.

A woman may have lost a baby. I could go to her, shed tears, and pray with her, but I wouldn't have the same sympathy and understanding as another woman who had lost a baby — and gotten through it.

That's why I believe God has called me to work with Vietnam vets — because, with God's help, I made it through my problems.

Opportunities to work with Vietnam Veterans began to come my way. I was asked to be the representative for the State of Missouri to the Vietnam Veterans of America convention — not because I was somebody, but because I was the only vet in our chapter who wasn't incarcerated.

With fear and trepidation, I went as a delegate to Washington, D.C., where I was exposed to hundreds of Vietnam veterans. During the convention, thousands of delegates met continuously, voting on laws and bylaws for the Vietnam Veterans of America organization.

For the first time, I realized why congressmen and lawmakers must compromise on political issues. I found that if I compromised on one issue, then I could count on the support of other people to pass a motion I felt more strongly about.

As I met and talked with other Vietnam veterans, my emotions were in turmoil as pain from the past came to the surface. I realized that there weren't just a few hundred of us — there were three million men and women who had served in Vietnam — and nobody that I knew of was reaching this group for Christ.

During the convention, an excellent band called "Britt Small and Festival" was playing in the hotel. When I discovered that Britt Small had been with my outfit in Vietnam, I decided to introduce myself. As he was coming out off the stage, I stopped him, and we talked for a few minutes. He was gracious and friendly.

That meeting began a long and lasting friendship with Britt Small and Festival. Since then, I have had the privilege of singing with them probably 100 different times around the country.

Later, I was invited to speak at the Vietnam Veterans of Iowa reunion, and sat with the governor and several other dignitaries at the head table.

Over the next few years I also met General Westmoreland and Congressional Medal of Honor recipients Kenny Stump, Al Lynch, Sam Davis, and Gary Weitzel. It has been a real blessing to work with these people and other American heroes and ex-POW's like Jeremiah Denton and Red McDaniels.

Several months after the Washington convention, I met a man named Shad Meshad, who had started the first walk-in vet center in California. A psychologist, Shad wrote the book *Captain for Dark Mornings,* which I recommend to any Vietnam veteran who wants to get the perspective of a Vietnam officer instead of a grunt. It exposes the turmoil and problems that the officers encountered. I learned a lot from Shad and his book.[1]

When I realized I would be evangelizing veterans all over the country and couldn't remain in one place, I decided to leave the church in Missouri. The Lord sent another pastor, and I began to travel.

Donna really wanted me to pastor a church. Since I had

spent so many years on the mission field, she thought we should settle down. After three years of being "settled down," however, I was going crazy.

The stress of the prison and the church finally took its toll, and I had a mild heart attack that forced me to take it easy for a couple of weeks. During that time, I realized that I couldn't be locked into one place any longer; I had to have room. "God has put something in my heart," I told Donna, "and I have to go."

When I heard about the second annual Vietnam Veterans Reunion in Kokomo, Indiana, I called and asked, "I was wondering if I could be on the program?"

They had heard of me and some of the things that I had done. My book, *Vietnam Curse or Blessing,* was out and doing very well. "Yes, we would be honored to have you be on the program," they told me.

During that weekend, veterans from all walks of life attended. As they came up to the entry gate, I walked over and asked them their names and what unit they served with. At first many were reluctant to talk about Vietnam.

They asked questions like, "Why did you come here?"

When I told them, they would say, "I have to go."

"Aw, come on in. You may find a buddy here," I suggested.

Some thought if a man talked about Vietnam and if he came to the reunion, maybe he had a problem — like the whining, crying Vietnam veteran that the media had stereotyped.

I literally pulled some of them through the gate. Later, when I would see the reluctant ones, they would be talking with a buddy or someone who had served in the same outfit with them. As they began to relate to one another, many were hugging each other with tears running down their faces.

As God opened one door after another, I had many opportunities to minister His love and mercy. My main ministry was simply hugging the vets and saying, "Thank you for fighting for your country."

The POW/MIA rally at the reunion drew about a

thousand people. At the Sunday morning program, however, perhaps only a hundred came. I spoke to the vets about Jesus Christ and how His love and forgiveness could heal the hurts and memories from Vietnam. As I sang, I could tell that the Holy Spirit was touching hearts. That meeting confirmed in my heart that this was what God had called me to do and where He wanted me to be.

That was 17 years ago. Now the reunion organizers anticipate my participation. Britt Small and Festival also come, and I sing with them. Every year, the church service at the reunion has grown. So many people now attend that no building can hold us on Sunday morning.

Most of those who attend don't go to church anywhere. They come to hear the Word of God and to be honored as soldiers. Why do we honor them? Because the Bible tells us to obey those who have rule over us "for they bear not their weapons in vain." It also states that soldiers are ministers of God.

Policemen, too, are like ministers of God. If we didn't have them, America would be in chaos. People complain about the corrupt police force and the corrupt military, but if they were eliminated, the guy with the biggest gun would be in control.

The veterans are important, and they're America's greatest asset. I lift them up, thank them, and tell them how I appreciate them. I tell them about another soldier, Jesus Christ, who paid the price. The Bible says, "That greater love has no man than this, that he will lay down his life for a friend." The only one who has laid down His life for me is Jesus Christ. And with His death and resurrection, He bought my salvation. I appreciate that!

Many Americans have laid down their lives for me, and if they hadn't, I wouldn't be alive today. That's why I appreciate the American veterans and want to be involved with them. Hundreds of veterans have made commitments to Christ — not by repeating the words after me, but by a change in their lives and by the commitments they have made in their hearts to Jesus Christ.

A few years ago, I had a message prepared, but the night before, the Lord told me to change it and to preach on suicide.

Generally when a Vietnam vet says he is going to commit suicide, he does. He sticks a gun in his mouth and pulls the trigger.

On separate occasions, I have counseled with two veterans who both have a scar over their eye. Each stuck a .22 in his mouth, and the bullet deflected off the roof of his mouth and came out above the eye instead of through the brain. These two guys were given a second chance from God.

The Scriptures teach that we are bought with a price, and we don't have the right to destroy our life. Who knows what goes through a person's mind in the last few seconds before he dies?

The Lord tells us to have patience with the feeble-minded. I know that God is a just God and that He will judge all. He knows the whole situation — not just the last moment.

I don't preach about going to hell after committing suicide. That's not my business. Instead, I tell vets that suicide is the most selfish act they could ever perform.

"Suicide makes me mad," I tell them. "Why? Because I'm the one who has to talk to the families about feeling guilty and wondering how they failed their husband or father. I'm the one who has to deal with the children who later decide to follow in their father's footsteps and commit suicide themselves." I don't pull any punches. I give them the facts.

Men hiding behind big, bushy beards with tears rolling down their faces have come up to me and said they were planning to commit suicide. "How did you know what I was thinking?" they ask.

"I've been there myself," I tell them.

After one service, seven vets came up to me and said they had been wanting to commit suicide and thanked God for the message. "I have been trying to kill myself with drugs and alcohol," one man said. "And I want you to walk to the dumpster with me."

"Why?" I asked, noticing he was carrying a beverage cooler.

"I want to throw away this beer," he said. "What you said really made sense to me. I don't want to do that to myself anymore. I believe now that I'm important. This country has a problem, but I'm somebody and God loves me. Jesus saved me today!"

"Let's go," I said and went with him. His wife and kids followed us, crying and rejoicing at the same time.

After one of my sermons, I received this letter:

Dear Brother John and Donna,

This is a hard letter to write, and I really don't know where to start. I guess the beginning is the best place.

Last Sunday morning at your Kokomo service was a very special day for my wife and myself. I don't mean to be selfish, but it seemed as if you were directing your sermon at me.

This past year has been one of those years that a person just wants to forget. But, Brother, the more I think about it, I don't know whether God is speaking to me or trying to teach me. Whichever it is, the Lord is trying to tell me something. Prayer is helping out a lot. Just maybe someday I'll understand. But for now, I'll keep working on it.

December 17, 1987, was one of the lowest days of my life. My father passed away just before Christmas. That was one day I wanted to end it all. My dad and I were pretty close, and I was just starting to open up with him. I had so much I wanted to tell him, but there just wasn't time. I know now that he knows, so I feel better about that. I sure miss him, but I know that he's in a much better place.

Several Christian brothers who really love me helped me through that difficult time. Then I started drinking real heavy and smoking pot again. I was depressed and turning into a real S.O.B.

Then my wife lost all control of her right foot and was having trouble walking. When I finally got her to the best specialists in this area, they were all buffaloed.

My wife is a nurse and had worked with this one doctor for about five years. He told us that he wasn't going to mess around with it and set us up with one of the top orthopedic surgeons at the Mayo Clinic in Rochester, Minnesota. What a place! They did all kinds of tests and found a tumor on the side of her leg.

Not knowing what it was, I was going nuts. Brother, I prayed more in that two days than I have in the last 20 years. I asked the Lord why He had to let something like this happen to someone who is such a beautiful, loving person. Well, I guess my prayers were answered because it was not cancer, and she is back to work and her foot is almost normal again. So all I can say is praise the Lord!

Another good thing came out of that trip to Minnesota. I ran into another vet and helped him through a problem he was having with his wife. There's nothing like "The Brotherhood."

Then my daughter had her turn. First, she got her foot run over by a car. Then she fell and broke some teeth. So, you can see things haven't been going too good.

Everybody is fine now except me. I have had more flashbacks and nightmares in the last six months than I have in the last 20 years. So, I tried to escape by using liquor and drugs, but it wasn't working. In fact, it was getting worse. Then I started fighting with my wife. We got into some pretty bad ones. I'd come home drunk and just looking for something to fight about. Thank God, I'd leave the house before I did something that I might regret.

My depressions were getting so bad that every time I'd drink, I would start thinking of suicide. At that time it seemed to be the only way out of the mess. I was tired of messing up everybody else's life.

Brother Mike and I had some pretty good talks.

Then on Sunday you really opened up my eyes. When you said, "Hold the one next to you," my wife and I embraced each other and cried. The look in her eyes told me she knew that I had been thinking about suicide. I have never told her of my intentions, but she knew. John, she is the most beautiful and understanding wife a guy could ever ask for. She still doesn't understand a lot, but she's trying. I truly love her with all my heart.

You'll be happy to know that it's Tuesday, and I haven't had a drink since Saturday night. I have made a promise to my daughter, to my wife, to the Lord, and to myself to lay off the drugs and booze. And I mean it!

In fact, this coming Sunday, we have been asked to attend and help set up a brand new church. We are looking forward to it.

Well, Brother, I have another letter to type. Thank you for your words Sunday. I feel you have helped to turn my life around.

One of my favorite songs of yours pretty well says it all, "You've Never Given Up On Me."

In God's Love,
Fellow Vet

Every year, I get excited about going back to Indiana. When I go back, some gal will run up to me, grab me around the neck, and start kissing me on the cheek. "What is the matter with you?" I'll ask.

"You prayed for my husband last year. Since then he has been taking us to church. He quit drinking and stopped beating me. Thank God," she will reply.

Men come up to me and tell me that they haven't drunk since the year before because God has touched their lives — and because they don't need it to survive.

One day a Vietnam vet came up to me and said, "I have cancer all through my body." He smelled terrible from the open wounds and looked 20 years older than he really was. I could tell that he was drinking pretty heavily.

He asked, "Brother John, would you pray for me to get saved?"

"Sure." I prayed and then led him to the Lord.

I didn't see him again until the next year's reunion. He still had cancer, even worse than before, but he said, "John, I became a Christian last year. My life has changed, but I can't take doing nothing any longer. I want some of your contacts in El Salvador so I can go there."

"Why?" I asked.

"Because I want to go down and fight against the Communists," he replied.

"Brother, why do you want to do that?"

He answered, "Because I am dying, and I want to die with dignity. I want to be killed there because I can't stand to die slowly like this."

"I would never give you that information because your motive isn't right," I told him "You have a responsibility to raise your family and serve God right here."

He was crying as he said, "But, John, you don't know what it is like. Some days I can't get out of bed, and they have to clean me up when I mess the sheets. I am a proud Vietnam veteran. My wife and kids have to help me walk sometimes and clean up my dirty body. They have to smell this stink from all the open wounds on me. I just want to get it over with."

"I want to tell you something," I said. "You don't

realize it, but you think you are going to do them a favor by getting out of the picture. You are just going to hurt them. You need to be strong until you die unless God does a miracle in your life. You need to let them help you and then, when you die, they can say to themselves, 'We really loved Dad and did all we could do to help him, and now we know he is at peace with the Lord.'

"If you take that away from them, then they are going to feel the same kind of guilt you felt when you came back from Vietnam — when your buddies died, and you didn't, and you couldn't help them. You need to give them the right to help you. If it means to help you take care of yourself until you die, then that is what you need to do."

When I saw him again the following year, he was doing better and had become very close with his family.

You may be wondering what could cause such a horrible case of cancer. I don't have all the statistics on Dioxin (agent orange), but I have seen many Vietnam veterans die of cancer that I believe resulted from Dioxin poisoning. The number of cancer deaths among Vietnam veterans is way out of proportion when compared with the rest of society.

Other vets haven't died but have had various operations to cut out different kinds of tumors from their bodies. I believe there must be a connection between cancerous tumors and Dioxin. Dioxin is the strongest toxin known to man, and it was dumped on us in Vietnam to kill the foliage of shrubs and trees.

※

The last man I dealt with at Kokomo was sitting on a bench crying. When I went up to him, he asked, "Can you help me?"

I said, "I hope so."

"John, I have been wanting to kill myself for a long time. I was a corpsman in Vietnam. When I saw something move in front of my position, I didn't know who it was. I shot and killed my best friend!"

To add salt to the wound, he named his first-born son

after that friend. Every day when he looks at that son, he is reminded of what he had done.

After the reunion, he was going to Washington, D.C. to visit "The Wall" — the Vietnam War Memorial.

I asked him "What if the role had been reversed, and your friend had killed you instead? Would you want that friend to ruin the rest of his life and his children's lives and feel guilty for it all these years?"

He said, "No, of course not."

"Your friend wouldn't want you to, either. What you did was a mistake. It happens. You can't undo it," I said.

"I'm going to The Wall to find his name," he told me.

"Instead of keeping this man alive in your mind, why don't you bury him when you go to The Wall? Lay him to rest. God forgave you the first time you asked for His forgiveness, and if you'll forgive yourself, you can go on with your life," I said.

As I held him, he cried and said, "John, I'm going to try."

Endnotes:

[1]Shad Meshad, *Captain for Dark Mornings* (Playa del Rey, CA: Creative Image Assn., 1982).

CHAPTER 16

The Wall

Y ou'll never guess who called today!" Donna said excitedly one day. My wife is the backbone of this ministry while I'm out on the road. When she is not with me, she is at home answering the mail, praying for veterans over the phone, and counseling people.

"Someone from CBN called and wants you to be a guest on the 700 Club."

"Great!" I replied.

"Maybe I could go along, too," she suggested.

"Honey, there is no way I am going to ask these people for two plane tickets," I said. "It is such a privilege that they are going to fly me there to do a program. Maybe some money will come in, and you can go. Let's pray for an extra $300 for another round trip ticket."

The next morning, Jackie Mitchem — the 700 Club guest coordinator — called and said, "John, I was praying and wondered if your wife would like to come with you. I felt impressed by the Lord to call you and ask you. We usually pay for only one person, but if Donna wants to come, we will send her a ticket also."

I said, "Praise God. That is what we have been praying for."

Donna and I flew to Virginia Beach and were treated like royalty. The folks at the 700 Club were very gracious and put us up at the Omni Hotel in a beautiful room overlooking the bay.

Since that first visit, CBN has continued to bless our ministry in many ways over the years.

The program was hosted by Sherri Lee Lucas. During the interview, we touched on some strong points about Vietnam, I was able to tell my story in capsule form. Afterwards, I was emotionally drained.

When Donna and I arrived back at the hotel, our phone was ringing. A squeaky little voice on the other end of the phone said, "Hi, my name is Lynn Hampton. I was a nurse in Vietnam and was on duty at the 93rd Evac in Longbien when they brought all the wounded in from Dak To." She was half crying.

My nerves were still raw from the program, and all I wanted to do was forget about Vietnam for a while. I thought, *Sure, you were, lady.* Since my return from Vietnam, a thousand guys have told me they were on Hill 875 when, in fact, there were only a handful of us who lived after that battle. *Why is she bugging me?* I wondered.

Then she said something that just about ripped my guts out. "All the bodies were rotten. The live ones and dead ones." Only someone who had been there could have known that.

We had been fighting in the jungle for five days. Some guys had been dead for five days, and some had been wounded for five days. We were lying out there with maggots and leeches crawling all over us and our open wounds. Our flesh was rotten. We had been in so much rain that our skin had shriveled up.

Her comment really touched my heart, and I started to cry.

"John, I have to meet with you. I have to talk to you," she said.

Frankly, I didn't know exactly what she meant, but I said, "Okay. I will be in Washington, D.C., next week speaking at a veterans gathering. You can meet me there."

She came to Washington, and we met and talked. For

six hours, she unloaded non-stop about Vietnam. "This is the first time anybody has been able to understand a little bit of what I have been going through," she told me.

A combat soldier sees a lot of death and pain — so much it can make him crazy. But nurses and doctors see only wounded and dying people for a whole year. They had to practice triage and decide who to take care of first — who lived and who didn't.

Lynn and I talked about her experiences. She was especially disheartened by the bureaucracy of the military and the people who were more concerned with their careers than with the life-and-death plight of the soldiers.

We instantly became very good friends. Donna and I "adopted" her as our little sister, and she has since been to our home many times. We also have visited with her and her precious sister Leigh in Florida. Lynn is now on our board of directors for Living Word Christian Ministries.

My appearance on the 700 Club opened up many doors for me. For the next five years I spent more time on the road than I did at home. That was hard on me, on Donna, and on the children. Now we are trying to find a better balance between the ministry and our home life.

As I got more and more involved in working with veterans, I ran across a song by Rheba Rambo, called "Wounded Soldier." The first time I heard it, I said, "Now there's a song for us." Although it was written with Christians in mind, the song reminded me of the emotional wounds suffered by Vietnam veterans.

It so touched my heart that I began to sing and share it with various veterans groups. I could see that the song was becoming a vehicle for the Lord to touch their hearts.

When I went out to the Festival's farm in Skidmore, Missouri, I planned to share the song with Britt Small and Festival, a popular band with veterans. I thought it would be great in their repertoire of music, thinking that Britt could sing it.

After setting up my portable sound system in their dining room, I sang the song for them.

Britt immediately said, "John, we've got a big program coming up in Washington, D.C. for the dedication of The Wall, and we'd like you to be the one to sing this song."

I couldn't believe what I was hearing. Me sing at the dedication? God certainly works in wonderful ways.

"That would be an honor and privilege," I told Britt. I had never expected to be present when President Reagan accepted the Vietnam Veterans Memorial into the national parks system.

The large stage where Festival and I were to perform was at the other end of the Washington mall. Frankie Vallee and the Four Seasons were on the same program with us, and I got to meet several Congressional Medal of Honor recipients — with whom I have remained friends over the years.

"Lord," I prayed, "give me a special anointing as I sing." I knew that an estimated crowd of 40,000 people would be listening.

As I looked out at the ocean of faces and began to sing, I almost panicked. I couldn't even hear my voice because of the background noise. The speakers were placed in scaffolding 40 feet high, and I didn't know if anything was coming out of them or not. Out in front where the people were, the music sounded fine.

Britt Small and Festival played for me, and the anointing of God was touching and moving the people. About halfway through the song, as I was singing the words, "Don't let a wounded soldier die," a man came up to the stage and reached up. He was trying to hand me his Purple Heart.

Holding the microphone in my other hand, I kept singing as I reached down with my hook, picked up the medal, and held it up to the crowd clasped with my hook.

The crowd was deeply moved, and many people were crying like babies as waves of love brought healing and comfort. It was truly a blessing for the 40,000 — and for me.

Since that day, I have sung with Britt Small and Festival and over the years we have worked many veterans reunions together and we have become great friends.

That night, after President Reagan spoke, we had a candlelight service at The Wall. That service unified our nation as many veterans received their first welcome home from another vet or another individual since they had returned to the States.

> The Vietnam Veterans Memorial, dedicated on Veterans' Day 1982, has become America's wailing wall. It is the place where family, friends, and buddies come to remember the 58,182 dead and missing whose names are engraved there on black granite panels.
>
> It is where Americans come to "commune" with the dead and the living and leave with a new understanding of the physical and emotional sacrifice of the Vietnam veteran. (*The Wall,* Copyright 1987, Collins Publisher, Inc.)

The dedication of The Wall changed my life and began a new phase of my ministry. Since then I have spoken over 50 times in Washington, D.C., including in front of the Reflecting Pool on the POW-MIA issue.

I have also seen much ministry take place at The Wall, as I have counseled with Vietnam vets, listened to their stories, and prayed with them. One day I was talking to a man who told me that he wasn't still upset over Vietnam, but that when he came back, he couldn't deal with his wife or his child and left them.

"Now," he said, "I don't have the courage to go back and apologize to her. So I sneak around the school grounds sometimes to get a look at my daughter."

When people come to The Wall, healing takes place. They come looking for the name of one of their friends or loved ones. When they find it on The Wall, many people have their own personal funeral service and finally bury that person — realizing that he truly is gone.

The first time I visited The Wall was at night with **my**

new friend Lynn Hampton. I went there to look for the name of Carlos J. Lozada, Congressional Medal of Honor recipient, who died in my arms on Hill 875.

I had been told I would find his name on slab number 30E, line 34. Slowly, but deliberately, I began running my hook over the lines of names counting line after line. Suddenly I saw the name of Charles W. Watters.

I thought my heart was going to pound itself out of my chest. "Father Watters, Father Watters," I sobbed. "You were such a brave man of the cloth and what an inspiration you were to all of us." Father Watters died in battle alongside his men.

I wasn't prepared for what happened next. The names are listed on The Wall according to the time the men died and not alphabetically. So, they came right at me, one after another: Jack Shoop, Harvey L. Brown III, Robert Bly, James Patterson, Jesse Sanchaez, Robert Szymanski, Jerome C. Shomaker, and there he was also — Carlos J. Lozada.

I reeled in remembrance and agony. As I continued to sob, I found myself talking to Carlos, saying, "Carlos, Shoop, and the rest of you guys, thanks for dying for me."

The "Hill" where they had all died loomed before me once again. I heard their cries, smelled the burning flesh, and saw their faces — hundreds of faces. Lynn comforted me with the love of Christ.

Looking into that black granite, those names became people and faces again. They weren't just names; they were personalities. This guy was overweight; that guy was always cracking a joke; this guy was so nice and kind; that guy was such a good fighter.

As the names became people again, I continued to cry and wondered, *Why am I alive and all those thousands of soldiers are dead?*

God then spoke to my heart and said, "John, I spared your life so that you could have the ministry that I have given to you."

It had taken me a lot of years to realize and accept that

God indeed has a ministry for me. He wants to use me to help other veterans who are still alive and suffering.

I don't have it all figured out yet, but I know that God is a faithful Father and He does have me here for a purpose. So rather than spend the rest of my life wondering why, I'm simply going to serve Him and make my life count for something.

Before I left The Wall, I made this promise to my buddies, "Your deaths will not be in vain."

CHAPTER 17

God, Union, and Liberty

John, if you could just go with me to El Salvador one time, you could really touch these soldiers' hearts." My friend Lynn Hampton was working in El Salvador, Central America with a medical team and was preparing for another trip.

"Let me think about it," I replied.

The Lord has opened the door for me to work not just with Vietnam veterans but with World War II veterans and Korean veterans, I told myself. Could it be that He now wants me to minister to combat veterans in another country?

Veterans of all kinds — and from all wars — were dealing with Post-Traumatic Stress Disorder — a problem affecting veterans who keep their stress bottled up inside themselves long after the war. As a result, some Vietnam vets just blew up and flipped out.

Only in the last few years has the public been concerned about Vietnam veterans and begun to identify some of their needs. I thought, *What an opportunity to share with the Salvadorian soldiers — to help them understand they don't have to feel guilty and ashamed the way society has tried to make the Vietnam vet feel.*

I told Lynn, "Yes, I will go." Several weeks later, I was on my way.

When I arrived in San Salvador, Lynn picked me up at

the airport and took me to a beautiful home up on the side of a mountain. The house belonged to the German embassy and had been rented by the ministry of Cuby and Jeanine Ward. This couple has spent many years doing the Lord's work there in Central America.

Lynn worked with the medical mission teams and went with doctors doing surgery and caring for the wounded. At times, I accompanied them, but my primary purpose was to minister to the soldiers - not only in the hospitals but also out at the military bases in the combat areas. I wanted to encourage them and share the gospel with them.

I hadn't been in the country too long when the ministry received a call from a lady who belonged to one of the five wealthiest families in El Salvador. At least that was the case before the government confiscated most of their properties and assets. This woman told us, "A note was put on the gate of my property saying that the Communist terrorists were going to kill me unless I give them $6,000 in cash."

The guerrillas who lived in town and worked as factory workers by day would put on their combat clothes, get their weapons, and sneak out into the mountains at night. Then they would terrorize the local people. "Many times I have seen them slipping through my backyard and going up into the mountains," she said.

We jumped into the van and went to her home where we prayed with her and praised the Lord. Then we said, "We'll stay with you tonight."

The guerrillas were supposed to come that night and kill her. We didn't have guns, and she didn't have any intention of paying the ransom. She was a widow and had already been fleeced by the government. We continued praying and waited for something to happen. She had a guard outside with a shotgun, but that wasn't much protection against automatic weapons and a whole band of Communist terrorists. Thank God they didn't come that night. We went back to our residence the next morning, and I left to speak at various military bases.

At one of the bases I was told that the Communists did

come the next day. Fortunately she was able, before they cut the phone lines, to call out and get the national police to come. They responded quickly. Several terrorists were killed in her backyard the very next day.

At first, the military treated me cautiously because so many "preachers" had told the soldiers, "Thou shalt not kill." Then after the preachers left, the officers couldn't get the soldiers to participate in defending their country.

Lynn Hampton and another friend, Anna Maria Estrata, talked to different military commanders they knew. I had also made friends with an American advisor, who told me, "Well, I'll try and get you in, but they are afraid you are going to turn these guys into pacifists."

When I got into the first base, I preached Christ to them. They had been told, "You can't be a Christian and be a soldier. When I asked them if they were Christians, most of them — having been raised Catholic — would say, "I was a Christian, and when I am not a soldier anymore, then I will be a Christian again. You can't be a soldier and a Christian." That statement really bothered me.

I started preaching to them out of the Bible and sharing with them that one of the greatest men of faith in the New Testament was a centurion soldier. Jesus healed His servant because the people said, "He is worthy, for he loves our country and he hath built us a synagogue."

I also told them "If it weren't for the American soldiers, the United States wouldn't have the freedom to worship in any church we choose. It is the same with El Salvador."

These soldiers — who were helping to keep the country free — had been told by a certain Christian faction that the Bible teaches, "Thou shalt not kill." Literally translated, it says, "Thou shalt not murder."

"If you like to kill, you are sick," I told the soldiers. "If you take pleasure in torture, then there is something wrong with you. However, when the enemy is in front of your position, and you know they are coming to take away your freedom — and want to replace it with an anti-God system known as communism — you have an obligation according to the Scriptures. "Hebrews 13:17 says, 'Obey them that have the rule over you.' In fact, your job is to shoot the enemy. Not to take pleasure in it, but to do your job as a soldier."

I asked, "Can you be an electrician and be a Christian?" They all said, "Yes."

I said, "An electrician has his tools. His black electrical tape, his side cutters, etc. Can you be a plumber and be a Christian?"

They all said, "Yes."

I then talked to them about the plumber having a pipe wrench, pipe putty, and other tools as a plumber. I mentioned to them several other professions. Then I asked, "Can you be a Christian and be a soldier?" I told them that not only can they be Christians and soldiers, but they can't be good soldiers unless they are Christians.

I asked, "Do soldiers have tools of their trade?" They all held up their weapons and began to understand that they could be soldiers and Christians at the same time.

The meeting was very rewarding because many of them then proceeded to make a commitment to Christ. Soldiers came up to me afterward and told me about things they had done and asked me if God could forgive them.

One thing I was trying to do then — and still do when I go to El Salvador — is to stop the young 16 to 20-year-old soldiers from having post-traumatic stress after the war. I try to prevent them from feeling guilty by explaining to them what the rest of the Bible has to say, not just one verse. Jesus said, "Having done all, to stand" (Eph. 6:13).

I often told the soldiers, "The Scripture teaches in 1 Timothy that the man who doesn't provide for his own family is worse than an infidel. I am sure that verse also means keeping the anti-Christ system of communism from taking over your country."

I taught them that if they had committed atrocities, which happens in all wars — if they had taken pleasure in torture or had killed prisoners — they should repent. "God will forgive you for your sin," I said.

My ministry in El Salvador was well-received, and I was honored by the military commanders who presented me with the flag that flew over the special forces camp at Chalatenango. Written on it were the words, "God, Union, and Liberty."

Many amputees have resulted from the war in El Salvador. In addition to the soldiers, civilian women and children were wounded by the Communists' mines planted at night in the roads.

During the war in El Salvador, the American media presented a biased picture in favor of the Communists. The reporters talked about the government death squads, but many of these assassins were actually Communists dressed up like Salvadoran soldiers.

The people of El Salvador knew the difference, but the press did not, and turned a blind eye to the truth. Even some liberal American church workers thought that America should get out of El Salvador and let the people be overrun by communism. Although the Salvadorian government has some problems, I believe it basically has a democratic format. When I shared with the soldiers on the bases, I encouraged them to continue to stand against communism.

Many in the military were starved for the simple, pure gospel of Jesus Christ that I preached: "If we confess with our mouth and believe in our heart in the Lord Jesus, we will be saved." I shared the gospel at 24 different military bases throughout El Salvador and saw hundreds of soldiers make commitments to Christ.

On one base I was speaking to 400 officer candidates who were halfway through the four-year program — one much like West Point. I shared with them how much God loved them and asked if any of them would like to make a commitment to Christ. I asked them without persuasion, without psychology, and without telling them they were going to get killed and go to hell.

Every one of them stood up immediately — 400 of

them, and made a commitment to Jesus Christ as a unit. I could hardly believe my eyes.

The commanders who originally didn't want me to come to their bases began to call other bases and say, "You have to have John Steer come and talk to your soldiers. He is putting into perspective and balance the fact that we do need soldiers — soldiers of integrity and honor, and not the kind who torture people and kill prisoners — those who are willing to kill only when confronted with the enemy."

ఴ

I visited the main hospital in San Salvador five or six times. It reminded me of the hospitals in Japan and in America after Vietnam, where many boys and young men — like myself — were recovering from their wounds.

As soon as I arrived, the hospital called out the amputees to the open area in the center of the hospital. I would share with them a little about my experiences in Vietnam and tell them how Jesus saved my life.

I realized that the soldiers of El Salvador respect the American Vietnam veterans much more than the American people do. Most of the training personnel in El Salvador have been ex-Vietnam veterans who have helped show them how to stay alive.

Many of these young men could not understand what had happened to their lives. One day they were strong, young Salvadorians and the next day they didn't have any legs. I could feel their pain and frustration. I knew they were wondering, *What will I do with the rest of my life? Will I survive?* When a soldier in El Salvador lost his legs or an arm, for instance, he was marked. When he returned to his village, the Communists tried to kill him sooner or later.

The Salvadorian military eventually learned to keep their wounded within the ranks of the military and give them some kind of job in spite of their handicap.

When I lost my arm in Vietnam and came back to the States and tried to stay in the military, the army said, "We don't want you."

I said, "I can save people's lives in Vietnam. I want to go to Fort Benning, Georgia, and train young paratroopers and infantry on how to stay alive in Vietnam and how to kill the enemy."

They said, "We don't want our young soldiers to see crippled, disabled veterans and to think that if they go over there, they might end up like you."

In Third World countries, people are taught that if they lose an arm, eye, or leg, they must become beggars since they are no longer worth anything. I told those young men, sitting around me in wheelchairs, "I fly an airplane and ride a Harley Davidson motorcycle."

Then I got out my guitar and took off my hook. Their eyes got wide, and they asked one another, "What in the world is this guy going to do now?"

Using a guitar pick built into a cup, I placed it over my stump and started to play the guitar. As I led them in Spanish songs and choruses, they all joined in jubilantly. The hospital staff told me, "These guys haven't laughed or had any fun in weeks." When I left, I knew I was also leaving behind hope.

On one of my trips, I met a minister who served as my interpreter. He had been an ex-Communist terrorist. Rene now has more zeal for Christ than he did for the Communist cause.

One day, Rene and I were ministering in the main hall of the hospital, where over 200 patients had gathered. Rene asked, "John, please sing, 'Wounded Soldier.'"

"Rene," I said, "they won't understand it, but I will sing it." The anointing of God surpasses the English or Spanish language. I began to sing, "The Wounded Soldier," and Rene translated the words into Spanish as I sang them in English.

The men cried and cried. They forced me — literally — to sing "Wounded Soldier" four times until I was crying so hard and was so physically and emotionally exhausted that I just couldn't do it anymore.

While I was singing, the Lord was saying to these men, "Somebody really cares about you and loves you. John Steer and Rene care about you. You, too, must love each other."

There is something very special about the camaraderie of soldiers. I have never had anybody in the church risk their life for me, but I have had soldiers die for me. They understood that. I prayed for the men, hugged them, and cried with them.

One man I prayed for had been paralyzed for three years. He seemed especially touched by our ministry. After I returned home, I received a letter saying that the man was sitting up in a wheelchair. Later, I heard that he was actually starting to walk with crutches. The power of the Lord had touched him. He had also been affected by the fact that somebody cared and gave him hope and the courage to try.

A young soldier named Pedro came up to me on crutches and, through my interpreter, shared with me that three months earlier he had his genitals completely shot off. Although he was not yet 20, this was the third time he had been wounded.

Pedro had a colostomy in his side and another tube to empty his bladder. The doctors had said they could do no more for him. "You have surgeons in America who can help me," he said. "They can even build me new genitals."

"I don't think so," I replied. "I've never heard of anything like that."

He disagreed. "Yes, I know that you do because I have read about it. Will you help me?"

I prayed for him and held him and said, "I won't promise you anything, but I'll check and see what we can do."

I shared his dilemma with Lynn Hampton, and she began to call around. She called Oral Roberts University.

I remembered that a week before I went to El Salvador, I had heard Oral Roberts on TV saying, "If you don't have the money, that is not a problem. Come in, we will take care of you. The City of Faith is a ministry."

Lynn called the hospital. I don't know who she talked to there, but someone said, "We'll help him. Get the proper papers and get him shipped here. We have surgeons who can work on his genitals."

A couple of days later, after we had started the ball rolling, the City of Faith called back and said, "We can't afford to help him. You are talking too much money, too much surgery. We're sorry."

That was a hard pill for me to swallow. However, God knows all!

Lynn then called the 700 Club and talked to Pat Robertson. Pat said, "I'll pray and get back to you."

Several days later he called and said, "We have two doctors in our church who are genital specialists. They are willing to donate their time. The 700 Club will pay the hospital bill and put the young man up while he is in the States. Don't worry. We will take care of him."

Lynn paid the air fare.

Pedro flew to Virginia Beach, and the doctors started his surgery as Pat had promised. He needed several operations. During one he died twice and was brought back to life. The surgery was very successful, and they put Pedro back together.

They told him, "You can have a normal married life, but, of course, you can never have children. If you had a twin brother, we could even make you fertile by taking one testicle from the twin brother."

It is amazing what God and science can do. Thank God for men of faith like Pat Robertson.

Pedro went back to El Salvador, where he is still a sergeant in the Salvadorian military. His goal is to tell people about two things: How great his God is and how He saved his soul. He also likes to tell how the Americans brought him to America for the creative surgery that restored his manhood.

I am just glad that I had a little part in bringing glory to God through Pedro's life.

In July 1990, I had the privilege of making a trip to the Soviet Union with the National Vietnam Veterans Coalition. We were a delegation of ten representing over 300,000 veterans. A friend of mine, Attorney Tom Burch, was chairman of the coalition.

We were hosted by the Soviet Afghan Vets — the Soviets who had fought in Afghanistan. Since they still had prisoners of war missing in Afghanistan and the Americans still had prisoners of war missing from World War II, Korea, and Vietnam, we had a lot in common.

After the war, their young Soviet soldiers were experiencing post-traumatic stress syndrome and blowing their brains out. The psychological problems were similar to those suffered by Vietnam veterans.

For ten days, we traveled the country, starting from the smallest town in the Urals where we were met by the mayor of the town. Along the way we were given larger meetings with more important government officials, until after ten days we ended up in the Kremlin with the prime minister, deputy prime minister, and general over all land forces.

While we were in the Soviet Union, we held many press conferences and were interviewed on television about the POW/MIA issue and the fact that we were concerned about over 2,200 Americans — many of whom are still unaccounted for from the Vietnam War.

We also expressed our desire for more information about 80,000 World War II veterans — of which 20,000 were known to be alive at the end of World War II, but were never returned. The same was true of about 8,000 Korean veterans. As proof, we provided documentation and facts, including government and secret files, concerning POW's, and the fact that the Soviet Union was still holding certain Americans.

We were all seated around the large horseshoe table with probably 30 generals in the room. When I was introduced as Rev. Steer, the general who was the highest ranking and was over all land forces — who had seen me on television and heard me sing — said, "Well, if we have a reverend here today, perhaps you should pray before we start the meeting."

It absolutely blew my mind. Behind me was a large bust of Lenin, and in front of me a general over the Soviet Union military was asking me to pray in the Kremlin.

So I prayed. I prayed for salvation for Russia, for all of us, for the meeting — and I prayed in the name of Jesus. Then I sang "Don't Let a Wounded Soldier Die," accompanied by my tape recorder. There wasn't a dry eye in the house.

That was an extremely moving moment for me. I realized that even Russians have a soul and that communism is really a facade because, in their hearts, all people know there is a God. They just need opportunity to hear the details, to accept Him, and to experience Him themselves.

***

At one press conference, I was sitting with the coalition members at a long table. Facing me were several Russian majors who had served in Vietnam and helped the North Vietnamese regular army. This made me very uncomfortable since I knew the medals the majors wore were probably gained by killing Americans.

One major mentioned that he was the head of a North Vietnamese artillery battery. My blood began to boil as I realized that same artillery was brought in against me and my men around the Dak To area in 1967.

While he talked, I had my hands in my pocket on a single blade case knife that I carried, and I kept snapping it open in my pocket. I thought, *If I jump up in a hurry I can get all four of these majors and cut their throats before anybody knows what happened.*

Then I would probably go to prison, I told myself. It took everything within me to quell the anger inside me as I confronted these men face to face who had once been my enemies.

As they spoke they said things that were really strange. One major said, "You know, you have a God in America that we don't have."

I thought, *How can this Communist soldier be talking about God?*

Then he starting talking about Bobby Powers, our U2 pilot who was shot down over the Soviet Union in the 1950s.

"It was my responsibility to shoot him down," he told

us. "At first, we mistakenly shot down one of our own planes, killing one of our own men. When we finally hit the U2, the plane exploded, and we presumed the pilot was dead. After the cloud of smoke cleared, a parachute blossomed and Bobby Powers landed safely in a field. I believe later we traded him for some Russian spies." That incident had made an impression on him, and he attributed Bobby Powers' rescue to the power of God in America.

Here I am, a minister, and I'm thinking about stabbing this guy, I said to myself, feeling ashamed. God softened my heart, and I was able to shake hands with the Soviet major afterward. It was another step in the healing process for me.

When I appeared on different Russian television shows, I would sing "Wounded Soldier." As I was singing, the Afghan soldiers who were hosting us appeared to be touched.

In the evenings, our delegation would sometimes go to a bar for something to eat. Some of the guys would have a few drinks, and the Soviet soldiers would be there. Someone would say, "John, why don't you sing something?" So I would stand up and sing, "God Bless the USA." Everywhere I went, I carried a tape recorder in my briefcase with background tapes to probably a dozen songs.

Then I would have an opportunity, through a translator, to share my testimony of how I suffered multiple wounds on three separate occasions. I talked about my combat experiences in Vietnam and how I spent a couple of years in the hospital. Then I would say, "And after all was said and done, I accepted Jesus as my Lord and Saviour, and that's the only way I can exist today. That was the only thing that could release me from the hatred and nightmares."

Afterward, many of the soldiers were very interested in Christ and were not ashamed to ask about Him.

Several times I went to the hospitals to talk with Afghan veterans who had psychiatric problems. I shared about Jesus and prayed for them. Even the hospital's chief psychiatrist said, "This Christian thing could be a good technique to help Russian soldiers." Of course, he didn't understand the value of a spiritual conversion and that there really is a God.

One day when I returned to the hospital to talk with the Afghan veterans, they had all gone home on leave. I said to the nurse, through my translator, "Well, don't you have any veterans in this hospital? Don't tell me they've all gone home."

She said, "All except the World War II veterans, and I know you don't want to talk to them."

"I would love to talk to the World War II veterans," I replied.

She said, "I don't know how we can get them all together. They're all up on the second floor."

I looked up and saw hallways going in every direction. I said, "Well, don't worry about it. I'll take care of it."

I went up to the second floor, opened up my briefcase, put a tape in the tape recorder, and started to sing "Don't Let a Wounded Soldier Die." The words and the music echoed throughout the high hallways. Suddenly, I had about 50 World War II veterans in the room with me and my translator.

The veterans began to ask me questions like, "How is God?" and "Where is God?" and "Is there still a God?" because I was introduced as a minister. They hadn't heard about God in 50 years.

I shared with them my testimony and how Jesus would save their soul. They all, without coercion or psychology or any tricks, were willing to hold hands with each other and willingly accept Jesus as their Lord and Saviour.

They gave me gifts. One veteran gave a man who had accompanied me his watch. One man gave me his medals. Since they lived in the hospital, the only valuables they had in the world were their medals from World War II. Tiny things that seem insignificant, yet that was all they had, and they gave them to us — because we brought them the gospel of Jesus Christ.

CHAPTER 18

Under Guard

W e lost six soldiers here yesterday," my military driver informed me. "The road was mined and they were killed." That wasn't unusual in El Salvador. We often saw fresh bullet holes in the ground or heard shooting. When that happened, the driver would take me in a different direction. Incidents like these often occurred on the many trips I continued to take back to this war-torn country. I am sure our lives were often in danger, but I didn't perceive it.

By this time, I had become fairly well-known on the military bases and was often asked to speak to the soldiers. During my first trips to El Salvador, I spoke at several churches, but that had changed.

The military was so grateful for my coming that they would find out where I was and would send a military driver to take me anyplace I wanted to go. I didn't have to rent a car or burden missionaries in the country with driving me around. The military driver always wore civilian clothes, had concealed weapons, and drove a civilian vehicle. Sometimes it would be a full-sized bus, sometimes a van, sometimes a small car. The military didn't want to draw attention to the fact that an American was encouraging the government soldiers against communism. If I were killed by the Communists, the Salvadoran military would have a major political problem on their hands.

To keep the enemy from monitoring my movements, my appointments were often changed at the last minute. They would announce that I was going to speak on this military base at 11:00 and then send me to a different base at 11:00 or to another one at 3:00.

I arrived at one base shortly after a Communist attack. Although the military had run them off, one Communist had been killed. He was still lying out in front of the base on the ground. About five people were wounded by the Communist guerrillas and had been taken to the aid station. When I saw the casualties, I walked into the aid station, laid my hands on the sick, and prayed for them.

The Latin people — particularly the El Salvadorian soldiers — are hungry for God and open to accepting Jesus Christ. After I had spoken at a movie theater packed with soldiers, an officer came to me and said, "I am responsible for over 100 men. People are starting to think that I am crazy, except for a few people in my unit who know I'm not."

I asked, "What do you mean?"

"When I went for training at the School of the Americas, Fort Benning, Georgia, mysterious things would happen. The door to my room would lock automatically. Objects would fly around the room. I was afraid. Nobody would believe me. Everybody thought I was crazy.

"After I completed the school and came back here to lead my men, I would hear a growling sound. I would ask if anybody else had heard it, and they would tell me no. They thought I was nuts. The hair would stand up on the back of my neck, and I would feel this terrible fear.

"The last time I was out on an operation, the growling sound was so loud and so ferocious that several of my men began running in the other direction. Suddenly, it was not just me hearing the growl. Everybody was hearing it. Brother John, is there any truth to demons?"

"If there is really a God, and I believe that there is," I answered, "then there really is a devil, and he has power to do such things."

"Please pray for me," he pleaded. "I want to be free from these demons."

I said, "First, let me ask you this: Have you ever accepted Christ as your Saviour? Do you believe that Jesus Christ died on the cross? Have you ever made a public confession that He died for your sins?"

"No," he replied.

"Well, would you like to do that?" I asked.

"Yes, I would," he said.

I prayed with this man to accept Christ and, as soon as I did, his whole countenance changed. I then rebuked the demons from tormenting him. The man turned to me and said, "Now I have something good to share with my soldiers. I'm not afraid anymore. I can tell them about this Jesus, who is really alive today. Now I can be a better commander." He went away happy and full of joy.

On another occasion, I was invited to go out to dinner with Colonel Jesus Casadis, a man highly respected by his people. Whenever a conflict between the military and civilians was brewing, he moved into these troubled areas.

In one of the cities that the military had recently taken back from the Communists, the people were scared to death. If they helped the government, the Communists could come back and retaliate. As a result, there was conflict between the military and the civilians. At that point, the government sent in Colonel Casadis, a very wise soldier and an excellent strategist.

Colonel Casadis sent his soldiers to work with the civilians, and together they painted all of the houses in the town white. Most of the houses had never been painted, making this a major improvement. When the people saw the soldiers working one-on-one with them, it brought healing in that area. The animosity between the soldiers and the civilians was defused along with the fear that the Communists would retaliate. The Colonel said, "John, the United States has the White House, and now we have the White City."

One evening when Colonel Casadis came to pick me up for dinner, he was riding in a little Toyota. As I went to open the door, it was so heavy I could hardly open it. The door must have weighed 400 pounds.

Once inside the car, I saw an Ouzi and some grenades at my feet. The glass in the doors was about five inches thick. I realized that I was in an armored car. I asked him, "How does the little Toyota motor pull this extremely heavy car?"

He said, "No es Toyota, es 350 Chevy, man." He had a 350 V8 Chevy motor in this little Toyota car.

Then I realized there was a car behind us and a car ahead of us, both with secret police in civilian clothes. As we ate dinner, these men positioned themselves in different places around the restaurant to keep us from being shot by terrorists.

"Not long before you arrived in the country, the Communist guerrillas shot down a helicopter carrying four Salvadorian generals," the colonel told me. "That is how the terrorists keep the war going. Instead of confronting an entire military base, the Communists assassinate political leaders and generals. They even burned a government office in downtown San Salvador. The building contained records for the sewers of the city and important civilian documents. That one act of terrorism created a bureaucratic nightmare."

It was difficult for me to enjoy my dinner, knowing that appearing with the colonel in public made us open targets for a terrorist attack. On the other hand, it was a great blessing to enjoy Christian fellowship with a fellow brother in Christ. As a strong Baptist, Colonel Casadis is a committed Christian of great integrity and honor. In fact, his influence opened the door for me to visit many military bases throughout El Salvador.

⌐⌐∎⌐

To get to the base located at El Paraiso, we had to use a small, private plane. I really enjoyed that trip, especially since the pilot allowed me to fly the plane. After we had been in the air for a while, I saw smoke off to my right and started heading in that direction. As I flew lower, the pilot said, "No," and he pointed in the other direction.

I said, "I want to see what's happening over here."

"A fire fight has been going on between the soldiers and the guerrillas for five days," he shouted. "Please do not get any closer. They have surface-to-air missiles."

He didn't have to tell me twice. I knew we could begin falling from the sky before realizing we'd even been hit. Immediately, I turned around and headed back toward our destination.

When we got to the base and landed the plane, the pilot shouted, "Hurry up and get out!"

"Aren't you going to stay?" I asked.

"No, I never stay here. They mortar this base all the time." The terrorists could hide in the surrounding hills and drop mortars on the base, which they did regularly.

As soon as the pilot pushed me out of the plane, he took off leaving me on the landing strip by myself. I didn't speak much Spanish, and to my knowledge no one on the base spoke English. I walked up to the first outpost where about ten soldiers were standing around a concrete bunker. After shaking hands and greeting them, I got out my tape recorder and sang four or five songs on the spot. They appeared to be touched by the music. "God loves you," I told them in what Spanish I knew and then moved on.

Since I was not scheduled to meet with Colonel Motovea until the next morning, I was taken to the only motel in the nearby town. Unfortunately, the motel was also a brothel with a line of about 30 men waiting to "visit" the prostitutes.

Looks like a captive audience, I said to myself. This is a good opportunity to meet some soldiers and talk to them. Using my broken Spanish, I talked to them about Jesus and gave each soldier a New Testament.

On that trip to El Salvador, I brought in 5,400 New Testaments and gave them out personally to all the soldiers.

Since the terrorists had destroyed many of the schools, children were being taught in temporary buildings without books or paper. I had brought in writing tablets with a Scripture verse printed on each piece of paper and thousands of pencils — also imprinted with a Scripture verse — for the children.

As I talked to the soldiers, I noticed bullet holes in the walls. "This motel was recently overrun by the Communists," they explained, "and most of the people inside were killed during the raid."

I was more than a little uneasy knowing that I was going to spend the night there with Communists just outside the city — and probably even in the city. My little concrete room had a window with no glass. It was just a hole in the wall with steel bars over it. The door was made of light sheet metal that anybody could kick in. A hammock and a canvas cot were the only furniture. I chose the hammock in which to sleep.

About midnight, I awoke in a horrible fright. Explosions! Before I could hear each explosion, I felt the waves of concussion going through my head. I knew it was close. I got on my knees and said, "God, You could have let me die in Vietnam. Why did You send me to El Salvador to die?"

Sweat was pouring off me as I struggled to keep my sanity. My mind was flooded with memories of Vietnam. I had a total flashback. When I came back to reality, I thought, *I don't have a weapon. I don't speak the language very well. I don't know who is my friend and who is my enemy. I'm probably the only American within 150 miles. What am I going to do?* The thought kept going through my mind, *They were here recently and killed all the people in the motel.*

I crawled up tight under the window, thinking that if they stuck a weapon through the window to clean out the room, I would try to pull it through the window and take it from them. I reverted back to combat mode. My muscles got tense, and I began to think of karate moves. *Man, I wish I had a weapon*, I said over and over to myself.

As I prayed, the Lord told me to relax, that He was in charge and I was not to worry. I tried to relax.

As I listened to the explosions, I heard four in sequence. "Boom, boom, boom, boom." It sounded like the same explosion from the same place each time. Then I realized that this was a sequence. These were not incoming rounds, they were outgoing.

Finally, I went back to sleep. The next morning I found

out that the motel was surrounded by 105 Howitzer cannons. During the night, terrorists had tried to come in from the mountains, so the military had called for a fire mission.

Later that day, I went to the base and was taken to the movie theater. About 700 soldiers had been assembled. Most were weary and tired, some appeared bloody and dirty, all were sweaty, and a lot of them were sleeping.

To get their attention, I spoke louder. When I began to talk about Vietnam and the experiences I had been through, they all perked up. I shared with them the precious message of salvation that was available to all of them. About halfway through the program, a colonel stood up in the middle of all the men and began to shout, "He's right. Listen to him!" This was the same man who had been leery of my coming on base the first time I went there.

After the meeting I was invited to a wonderful dinner with Colonel Motovea in the mess hall. The meal consisted of minnows, heads on, stir-fried, and about half-cooked — and they gave me a big pile of them. So as not to insult them, I ate the little critters, but it was hard keeping them down.

On one of the trips to this base, Lynn Hampton accompanied me. From there, we traveled to a hospital deep in the jungle where I talked to many wounded soldiers and counseled with them. In one ward, six teenage solders — about 16 to 17 years old — had shot themselves because they were afraid and wanted to avoid combat. I asked them, "How did this happen to you?"

"We were climbing a mountain and the gun went off," they answered. Realizing they were scared and needed the love of Christ, we ministered to them and loved them.

Since I had other military bases to visit, Lynn stayed behind and headed out into the Communist-held territory with the medical team to treat the sick, the wounded, and the children. I have tremendous respect for Lynn and the work she's done in the name of Christ in places like El Salvador.

Let me share with you about a friend I met in El

Salvador. I will not give his real name — I'll call him Jose. He has become a very dear friend and now is a minister of the gospel. For ten years, Jose was a Communist terrorist. Maybe if I explain how he became a Communist and how he got out of it, you'll be a little wiser to the deception that you read about in the press.

As a college student, Jose was majoring in chemistry. The Communist party, which was active on the campus, began brainwashing the students about the faults of the Salvadoran government. Obviously all governments have some faults. Day after day, they harped on the many social problems and hammered away at the government's unfairness until they convinced Jose that communism was the answer. Communism was supposed to be by the people, for the people, to help the people.

The Communists quickly learned that their greatest allies were the hundreds of American reporters who were covering the war. Jose would go to the President Hotel in El Salvador and find an American news reporter sitting at the bar. In many cases, the reporter was getting his news from a bar stool and not out in the field. "We're going to blow up the communications system in downtown San Salvador," Jose would tell him. By this time, the young chemistry major was making bombs for the terrorists to use.

The reporter would usually say, "I don't believe you; don't bother me."

Then Jose or another person would blow up the system. When he returned the next day, Jose had the reporter's attention. "Tomorrow, we're going to burn up a building at such and such a place," he would say. "If you want to get a good story, get out there and you'll see it happen."

The news reporter would think, *I'm not sure if they're really going to do that or not, and besides, I'm pretty comfortable at this bar. I think I'll stay here.*

The next day, they'd burn the building, and the reporter would find out. Then the reporter would say, "Man, I've got me a hot informer, and I'm going to utilize him. I'm not going to mess up again."

Then Jose or another terrorist would say to the reporter, "Tomorrow we're going to show you how the Salvadorian military kills women and children. We have information that they're coming into a village, and they're going to kill all the people." Now Jose had the reporter's undivided attention, and he knows he has a scoop. In the meantime, the terrorists have been working for six months to set up this scheme.

They have sent terrorists into a village where they made friends with the Salvadorians by playing basketball with the teenagers. At the same time, they have instilled fear in the teenagers by saying, "The Salvadorian soldiers are going to kill you guys."

The teenagers reply, "Our brothers are soldiers. They aren't going to kill us. This isn't true." Over a period of six months, the terrorists establish credibility with these young people, convincing them that an attack on the village is imminent. Then, when the terrorists tell them, "Here, take these weapons to defend yourself when the Salvadorian government comes in and tries to overrun you," the young people take the weapons.

In the meantime, professional terrorists slip into the nearest military base and kill half a dozen soldiers. They leave information that a nearby village is filled with Communist terrorists. The Communist college students then persuade the American press to set up their cameras on a hill above the village. When the angry Salvadorian soldiers go into this village that is supposedly filled with Communists, the young people panic and start to shoot. Then, with cameras zooming in on the attack, the Salvadorian soldiers kill all the young people in the village.

The press then labels the Salvadorian army as a bunch of baby-killing, no good soldiers, when, in fact, the whole scenario was orchestrated by the Communist terrorists.

My friend Jose told me that he had twice helped arrange such a scheme. Most Americans were unaware of the biased — and sometimes dishonest — reporting carried out by the media during the war in El Salvador. A missionary living in El Salvador, however, told me about an incident that happened at the President Hotel in San Salvador. "We watched as some members of the American media went out behind the hotel with their video camera. The reporter stated on camera that he was reporting from a different city in El Salvador. As he talked, he and the camera man pretended they were dodging bullets. Then he stated as fact the lies the terrorists had told him in the bar. The video cassette was sent back to America and was televised on the evening news."

I was shocked at such blatant deception, but at the same time not too surprised at the media's liberal bias.

After Jose had been involved in the Communist Party for ten years, he told me that he began to rethink his position. "We were doing things worse than what we were trying to stop. I became a Communist to help humanity and make my country a better place, but I was doing things that were much worse than anything my government was supposedly doing."

Shortly thereafter, Jose became a Christian and gave his heart to Jesus. As a believer, he knew he could no longer be a terrorist. When he tried to leave the Communist Party, his life was threatened. At that time he was dating the daughter of the highest-ranking Communist official in El Salvador. Jose took a stand and broke off the engagement.

By the grace of God and a miracle, Jose is no longer hunted by the Communists or by the Salvadorian government. In fact, he now speaks at military bases and brings the gospel of Jesus Christ to the soldiers.

Many of the boys who are Communists are not hard core. Many were kidnapped off the streets and taken to Communist camps where they were brainwashed and told, "You're going to fight with us, or we will shoot your mother or your kids." The only way some of these men could escape communism was to leave the country. They couldn't go to the military because somebody who knew them might shoot them. To help fleeing men get into other Central American countries, a network was established, making it possible for them to lead a normal life with their wives and children. If they refused to become Communists and stayed in El Salvador, they would probably be killed — and many were.

CHAPTER 19

Wake Up, America!

In 1993 I was at the Melbourne, Florida, Vietnam Veterans Reunion where I go to speak every year and do a concert. I also work with the veterans and do a chapel service. After the chapel service I was standing out back among a bunch of veterans. A guy came up and stood behind me and said, "John Steer?"

I said, "Yeah," and I turned around.

He said, "No, you're not."

I said, "Excuse me?"

He said, "You're not John Steer. He's dead." It was almost as if he was accusing me of impersonating someone.

I said, "Well, I hate to disappoint you, but I'm John Steer." I began to look at him and, with my mind, separate a few of his wrinkles, and his weight, and add a little hair to him. Then I asked, "Peanut, is that you?"

He said, "Yeah," and began to grin and wipe away a tear.

I said, "Well, you're dead, too. You were shot in the chest and in the stomach."

He said, "Yeah. But I ain't dead neither." We hugged and have been friends ever since.

When I share my testimony at churches, I often talk

about being wounded on three separate occasions, about the blood and guts of Vietnam, and the stories of some of the men and women I have counseled. Afterward, someone will usually cringe and ask, "Why are you talking about the war here at church? I didn't do anything."

I then explain, "Peter didn't do anything either when Jesus was in the courtyard, and they were whipping and spitting on Him. Yet Peter was within eyeshot of Jesus when the servant gal came up to him and said, 'You're one of them, too.' Peter said, 'I didn't do anything.'

"Perhaps you didn't do anything and maybe the church hasn't done much to help others, but it's time that we do!"

Other people will tell me, "Why don't you Vietnam vets pull yourselves up by your bootstraps, like your daddies did after World War II and Korea — and get on with your life?" How can people think like that? Apparently, they don't know what goes on in the minds of veterans. Anyone who takes the time to visit a VA hospital will find the beds occupied by veterans from World War II, Korean, and Vietnam. The psychiatric wards are full with veterans of all ages.

The problem with Vietnam veterans is not a new problem, but we have received more media attention. All veterans who have been in combat have had a lot of adjustments to make afterwards.

The question I would like to ask is: "Where is the church?" Where is the church that handed us the Gideon New Testament when we got on the train to go off and "Kill a Commie for Mommie"? The church was there to pat us on the back and send us off to war, but when we came back, no one showed up. When we came back, we didn't look like them, smell like them, act like them, walk like them, or talk like them — so we were not welcome in most churches.

Thank God, after all these years, churches are once again beginning to open up their hearts to the veterans!

※

Crazy J, at one time one of the leaders of Vietnam Veterans Motorcycle Club, heard me speaking from the back of an army truck in DeQuoin, Illinois, several years ago at a veterans reunion and a POW and MIA rally, sharing how the Lord had intervened in my life and helped turn me around.

When I had finished speaking, Jay came up with his K-bar, a Marine fighting knife, and surrendered it to me. Jay was a combat veteran and had been wounded. "I feel like God is talking to me, and I want you to have this," he said. I could understand where he was coming from. He was laying down his old way of doing things and trying to take on a new life.

I told him, "I'll be preaching in a church tonight not far from here. Why don't you come with me?"

Jay had his Vietnam Veterans Motorcycle Club leathers on and said, "John, if you will ride your motorcycle to church, then I'll ride mine and go with you."

I replied, "Sure, we will ride together."

I am proud to say I am also a member of the Vietnam Veteran's Motorcycle Club. When I go on the road in the summer, I pull my motorcycle in the trailer behind the vehicle. But I don't usually ride it to church. There I was in a three-piece suit riding alongside Jay in his leathers.

On the way to church I was praying, "God, let there be some Christians in this church. I don't care what the handle is above the door, just bring some Christians who care about our American veterans and our fighting men."

When we got to the church, about half the congregation came over and gave Jay a hug and said, "Thank you for fighting for our country, and welcome home, brother."

That really touched his heart.

Nineteen years earlier, when Jay had come home from Vietnam, he picked up his Harley Davidson in California and headed for Iowa. Jay drove a couple of days and all night so he could get home to go to church on Easter Sunday with his mother. He made it, but he was a few minutes late.

After parking his motorcycle in front of the church, Jay started up the steps to go into this big Catholic church and find his mother. Some of the ushers (whatever they call themselves) met him at the door and said, "You're not coming in here dressed like that!"

As a result of that one incident, Jay hadn't been to church in 19 years. Thank God we found a church where there were some Christians who cared.

≈▮≈

"Why don't you pull yourself up by your bootstraps?" That phrase wouldn't work for a young man whose wife had called me a dozen times. "My husband lives in Kansas City. Please help him," she pleaded.

I called him and told him I was coming to talk with him. He said, "I can't talk to you unless you let me drink. I can't talk about Vietnam unless I'm half-drunk."

I replied, "Go ahead and drink." I stayed up with him two days and one whole night before he finally started to unload about Vietnam.

"I was only 18 when I became a marine," he began. "When I arrived in Vietnam, I saw grass hutches and several people with weapons. I zeroed my rifle in on what looked to be about a ten-year-old girl. She was carrying an AK-47.

"I shot her in the chest," he said, sobbing. "She fell down into a stream, and the water washed her down into a rice paddy."

"The fire fight lasted only a couple of seconds, and some on both sides were killed," he continued. "As soon as the bullets stopped firing, I ran down the stream and into the rice paddy to find the little girl. I pulled out her limp, broken body with a big hole in her chest and sat her up against a tree. Then I started straightening up her clothes and primping her hair.

"My buddy came along and asked, 'What the hell's the matter with you?'

"I answered, 'I didn't want the little girl to drown.'

"She was dead, of course."

Now why doesn't he just pull himself up by his bootstraps? Why is he still having trouble 20 years later?

This Vietnam vet now has a daughter about ten years old, and every time he looks at her he sees that little girl he shot in Vietnam. Somebody says, "Why don't you just forget it and go on with your life?"

John Boldrey, a good friend of mine who is on my board of directors, lives in Kansas City. His wife used to call and ask, "John, please come and talk to my husband. Things are really bad. If things don't change, I am going to get a divorce. John really gets crazy. He gets drunk all the time, and is suicidal. Please come and talk to him."

I went to visit him. Before the night was over, we ended up wrestling on the floor like a couple of old dogs. John let it go that night and gave Vietnam, along with his hatred and anger to the Lord. Today John is in the ministry.

It's easy to say, "Why don't you just forget it?" Without God's help, however, it's not easy to forget. Even with God's help, the vets won't forget it, but they can put it into proper perspective and turn it around and use it for something good.

A man in North Carolina kept calling me. He has a hole in his arm and one in his back from which black fluid constantly oozes. He has a lot of problems and lives in low-income housing. In order to have bread and milk money for their two children, his wife works 80 hours a week taking care of an old lady and gets paid $50.

This man wasn't receiving any disability payments because every time he would file a claim, he would end up getting angry and not follow through. Many Vietnam vets who tried to file a claim weren't competent enough or were too bewildered to follow through with it — and little assistance was available to help them.

That was this man's case. The DAV had filed a claim for him, but he got angry and changed his power of attorney to the American Legion. Then he got mad at them and changed to the VFW. With all the confusion, his papers had not been filed correctly, and he wasn't receiving any aid.

As I was talking to him, I asked, "Are you a drug addict?"

"No, Brother John, I just take a few pills — just what the VA gives me. That's all I take," he answered.

His little daughter, who was sitting in the room at the time, started crying and said, "Daddy, you know that's not true. You take pills all the time. You're sitting on a great big bottle of pills right now under the cushion of the couch." I made him get up and looked under the cushion. There was a bottle filled with "downers" — anti-depressants. The man was a drug addict.

For the first time, he confessed, and we prayed that God would set him free.

I then called the service organization and told them the problem. "Look, man," I said to my friend, "you've got to stay with this service organization and not be changing your papers and power of attorney." Today the man is getting a modest pension and putting his life together.

Somebody said, "Why didn't he just pull himself up by his bootstraps?"

I was ministering in Pittsburgh, Pennsylvania, a few years ago when an old World War II veteran came forward and said, "I hate the Japanese. I can't help it. I hate them, but I want to quit hating them. Can you help me?" We prayed, and the man was freed from his hatred of the Japanese.

At the same meeting a Vietnam veteran came forward and said, "I hate the Vietnamese. I don't know why. I just hate them. Is there help for me?" After he gave his heart to the Lord, I prayed with him, and he was set free from this hatred.

Then a young lady came up and said, "I was married to a Vietnam veteran, and he committed suicide. Could you talk to me?"

Often we want a quick-fix answer at the altar. Instead, I said to her, "Let's go across the street to the restaurant and have some coffee and talk."

She had re-married and asked her husband if it would be all right, and he said okay. We talked for several hours.

She said, "When my husband came home from Vietnam, we got mixed up with the Mexican mafia. We lived in California and were dealing heroin. As a result, we both became addicts. One day there was only enough heroin left in the house for just one fix."

She paused for a moment and took a deep breath. "I told my husband that I was going to take the last of the heroin," she continued. "He began to scream at me. I then went and got the .357 magnum and stuck it in his face and said, 'If you don't let me take the last of this drug, I'm going to blow your brains out!.'

"John, he just laughed at me and said, 'After Vietnam, do me a favor and blow my brains out.'

"I got mad, started crying, and threw the pistol down. He then picked it up, and I said out of spite, 'If you had any guts, you'd do it yourself.'"

She paused for a moment before continuing. "He stuck the pistol in his mouth and pulled the trigger."

Somebody said to this young lady, "Why don't you just forget it and go on with your life?"

It doesn't work like that. It takes time. Hurting people need somebody to love them and work with them — somebody who really cares.

⌐Ⅱ⌐

When I was pastoring the church in Moberly, Missouri, a Vietnam veteran came into the church and wanted to talk to me. One of the deacons met him and hugged him.

The vet said, "You'd better get away from me."

The deacon found me and said, "Brother John, it's another one of them."

I said, "Tell him to go into my office, and I'll talk to him later."

Instead, he stayed in the sanctuary. From the pulpit, I could see the defiance in his face. When everybody else stood up, he sat down. When the congregation sang, he kept his lips buttoned tight. I could feel his bitterness and hatred.

After the service, he and his ex-wife wanted to talk to me, so they went into my office. He started hollering and cussing and said, "You know nothing about nothing."

I hollered back, saying, "Yes, I do, and I know where you're coming from. I, too, have been down that road."

He got mad and cussed me again and stormed out of the

church, slamming the door behind him. As he was leaving, I yelled out to him, "If you ever want to talk about it, morning, noon, or night, just call me."

I don't know why, but it seems like everyone in trouble always calls at two or three in the morning. He called, and I met him at an all-night restaurant. He began to share with me about the people he had killed, not only in Vietnam, but also in the United States. He had been in the Special Forces.

I thought, *This sounds too much like a James Bond movie to be true, but the man keeps giving me names, dates, and places.* It was obvious he had serious problems. Later, I ran a computer check on him through some sources I had at a police department, and it came up "censored by the FBI." Apparently the man was who he said he was.

He couldn't talk to anybody about anything he had done, but he talked to me in total confidence. To carry around that guilt and not be able to share it or be able to get any credit for what you've done is pretty tough.

A few weeks later, Donna and I were in Europe ministering the gospel on several American and Canadian military bases in Germany, France, and England. At one point in our trip, I was out at a camp at Boden-Boden, Germany, staying with a friend who was a sergeant in Special Forces.

While there I got a call in the middle of the night from this guy back in the States. Somehow he found out where we were and tracked me down. "My wife's been in a motorcycle accident that put her ribs through her lungs," he sobbed. "And her skull cap is broken in seven places."

I didn't know what to say.

"John," he pleaded, "I want you to get on the next jet and get home here. You're the only person I have any confidence in. Get home right now!"

"I can't," I replied. "We are here on a military hop, and we have to take the hop home. It will take two or three days minimum to get home. Even if I had the money, I can't come now, but God can surpass all of the boundaries. Let's pray for your wife right now."

The Special Forces sergeant, my wife, and I got down

on our knees, early in the morning, and prayed.

Four hours later we got a call back: "She is going to make it, but she may be a vegetable," we were told. We kept praying, and a short time later we found out that her condition was improving.

When we came home from Germany, I looked her up. She was doing fine. The Lord had touched her, and everybody was amazed.

Her husband said, "Well, I want you to know that I did it."

"You did what?" I asked.

"You know, I did IT. You know what I mean."

"You mean you became a Christian?"

He said, "Yes, and her dad did it, too."

"Well, praise the Lord!" I exclaimed.

Then he said, "John, I want to do what you do: tell people about Jesus." Here was a hard-core ex-Green Beret who gave his life to God because his wife was touched by the power of the Lord. This man began to talk to others about the Lord. His testimony has had a far-reaching effect. When he visits The Wall in Washington, D.C., he often tells vets who need help to call me.

One of these men did call me and said, "This Special Forces guy said I should talk to you. I've got problems."

I asked, "What's your problem? Are you a Vietnam vet?"

"No, but I've told people for 20 years that I was," he said, obviously ashamed.

"Twenty years ago I was assigned to the Marines to be a combat medic. I went to the third deck of the ship, crawled on the outside of the railing, and threatened to commit suicide until they told me I could have an 'unable to cope with the military' discharge. All I wanted to do was get out of the Marines.

"Later, I felt guilty after many of my friends went to Vietnam and were killed. So I began telling everybody that I was a Vietnam vet."

I said, "You were really smart at age 18 and thought you

WOUNDED SOLDIER

knew everything, didn't you? Let me tell you something. What you did was wrong, but I want you to know that I forgive you. Why don't you forgive yourself and pick up the pieces of your life and quit lying about it?''

He thanked me and hung up the phone. I'm sure he put his life back together again because all he needed to know was that somebody and God forgave him.

Since then, I have dealt with several people who have said that they were Vietnam veterans because they felt guilty that they didn't go.

One dear friend was a SEAL. He went through extensive aquatics and deep-sea diving training along with two other SEALS. One got killed in Vietnam, and one came home badly wounded and eventually died of cancer. This man, although he volunteered on several different occasions, was not sent to Vietnam.

Years later, he started hanging around with Vietnam vets and began telling the stories of his friends. He was found out by other Vietnam vets who checked out his DD2-14, and they totally ostracized him.

On the other hand, I met a man named Guzzi, a Catholic brother, and a baby Christian who wanted to share what he knew about Jesus. Guzzi spent a lot of time around Vietnam veteran groups, and they assumed he was one of them. As time went on, he started telling the same stories they were telling. Later, he became convicted of his lying and went to them and said, "I'm not a Vietnam vet. You assumed that I was, and I let you. I then started telling your stories. I'm sorry for lying about it, and I still want to be your chaplain and work with you." Everyone in that room forgave him, and he is still their chaplain.

In Luke 10:25-37, we read:

> On one occasion an expert in the law stood up to test Jesus. "Teacher," he asked, "what must I do to inherit eternal life?"
> "What is written in the Law?" he replied. "How do you read it?"

He answered: " 'Love the Lord your God with all your heart and with all your soul and with all your strength and with all your mind,' and 'Love your neighbor as yourself.' "

"You have answered correctly," Jesus replied. "Do this and you will live."

But he wanted to justify himself, so he asked Jesus, "And who is my neighbor?"

In reply Jesus said: "A man was going down from Jerusalem to Jericho, when he fell into the hands of robbers. They stripped him of his clothes, beat him and went away, leaving him half dead. A priest happened to be going down the same road, and when he saw the man, he passed by on the other side. So too, a Levite, when he came to the place and saw him, passed by on the other side. But a Samaritan, as he traveled, came where the man was; and when he saw him, he took pity on him. He went to him and bandaged his wounds pouring on oil and wine. Then he put the man on his own donkey, took him to an inn and took care of him. The next day he took out two silver coins and gave them to the innkeeper. 'Look after him,' he said, 'and when I return, I will reimburse you for any extra expense you may have.'

"Which of these three do you think was a neighbor to the man who fell into the hands of the robbers?"

The expert in the law replied, "The one who had mercy on him."

Jesus told him, "Go and do likewise."

When I share this story of the Good Samaritan, I relate it to America's veterans, lying in the mud, the blood, the guts, and the beer — veterans who are sleeping on the sidewalks of our nation's capital. If you go to The Wall in Washington, D.C. in the dead of winter with four inches of snow on the ground, you will find American veterans from World War II,

Korea, and Vietnam, trying to stay warm by sleeping on pieces of cardboard over the subway grates. I wonder how many pious Christians walk by them every day.

This parable tells of a man bleeding and dying by the side of the road, and a priest walks by. I can picture in my mind a priest, no matter what denomination, with long flowing robes and maybe a 14-pound solid gold cross around his neck. He thinks he really looks good, but he has been having trouble with his heart. Perhaps he went to his doctor and said, "Doctor, I have this heart problem."

The doctor says, "You need to walk every day."

He picks out the nicest trail in the city, through the Washington, D.C. mall area. As he is walking, he's smelling the flowers and listening to the birds and feeling the sun on his face. When he sees a veteran lying on the path, he says, "How dare you have the audacity to bleed all over this trail? I paid my taxes. Why doesn't the government take care of people like you? Why don't they put you someplace where we don't have to look at you?"

Then the Bible says he continued on his way.

I have personally encountered that same attitude in the church. In other words, "If you don't act like me, then I don't want to deal with you. If you don't pay your tithes here, then I'm really not interested."

Then there is the other extreme, the Levites. Ordained by God to take care of the tabernacle, they inherited their ministry as members of the tribe of Levi. You might say they were extreme "word" people. They lived by the letter of the law. We've got people today whom I would put in that category. They can't walk anywhere, they run around with their hands in the air all the time. They can say only a few words, like "Praise the Lord, Praise the Lord!"

One of them was skipping along one day and came upon this veteran who was bleeding and dying alongside the road. The Levite said, "Praise the Lord," and started to leave. Then he said to himself, "Maybe I'd better do something." So he turned around, looked at the veteran, and said, "Be healed in the name of Jesus." And he skipped on down the road, thinking to himself, *I'd better hurry. I don't want to be late for church.* When he got to church, they were having a testimony service, and he waved his hand and said, "Pastor, I have a testimony."

The pastor asked, "What is it, my son?"

"Today on my way to church, I saw a Vietnam veteran lying along the road bleeding and dying, and I told him to be healed in the name of Jesus."

The pastor asked, "Well, was he?"

The man said, "Pastor, I can't believe you said that. That's a negative confession. Of course he was, I think."

Then we have the Samaritan. He had something that Jesus called "compassion." I believe that Jesus lives in the mud and blood and guts and beer. I believe that God is a God who cares where you are and goes right to where you hurt. You don't have to clean someone up to come to God. God comes to them! That's what I believe God is calling us to do.

The Samaritan came by, saw the veteran, had compassion, got down on his knees, and bound up the man's wounds. Then he poured oil and wine on the sores, put him in his new car, and took him to the hospital. He then told the doctor, "Here's some money, and if that's not enough, let me know, and I'll pay you the balance when I return."

It is time for the churches of America to wake up and realize that for 200 years they have enjoyed freedom to worship God because soldiers and veterans have spilled their blood and given their lives to keep this nation free.

If there ever was a mission field, it should be helping the American veterans. If anyone in this country should get one, two, or three breaks, it should be the American veterans. They need to know Jesus and His salvation that we enjoy.

⛨

"John, I need to talk — and I need prayer," he told me. "In fact, I have never shared this with anyone before."

I prepared myself to listen.

"I was the first one on the scene when an American helicopter was shot down," he told me. "The North Vietnamese soldiers had already been there. The two survivors had been tortured, and the gooks had cut most of their skin off and left them alive to be eaten by the ants and die a slow and painful death."

He paused for a moment to regain his composure. Then he continued. "John, they were screaming in agony and were seeping blood everywhere. There was absolutely no hope for their lives. So I raised my M16 and shot them, and put them out of their torment."

Then people say, "Why don't you just pull yourself up by your bootstraps?"

Hank, another vet, came to me a while back for counsel. He was a guard at an amusement park. He had been in Vietnam with the marines in a Recon outfit. "John, all I can remember is that we were out on a mission, and some B-40 rockets landed by us," he began. "I don't know how long it was before I came to, but when I did, my friend and I were in a cage being carried through the jungle. For the next several days I was repeatedly sodomized by the North Vietnamese. How I prayed that I would die, but I didn't.

"Finally, I killed a guard and escaped. When I got back to the friendlies three days later, my superiors didn't even believe my story. I was ordered back to my outfit to finish my 13-month tour in Vietnam. John, I can't go on living."

And somebody says, "Why don't you just forget?"

Another veteran friend of mine had an interesting but painful experience when he came home. Joe, a Green Beret, returned from Vietnam after a year's tour of seeing a lot of combat and brutality. He arrived home in the middle of the night. His parents lived in a two-story house. Joe had drunk a few beers, and he was banging on the door for his parents to let him in. They opened the window upstairs and yelled, "Who is it?"

Joe answered, "It's me, Joe, your son. Let me in!"

"Come back in the daylight," they replied.

He hung his head and walked away. Joe hasn't been back to see his parents — and that was 30 years ago.

Somebody says, ''Why don't you just forget Vietnam?''

In some cases, it would be easier for us to forget it if this country could forget it. If our families could forget it. Unfortunately, no one will ever forget it until it is dealt with in individual's lives.

WAKE UP, AMERICA

Wake up, America, you don't even know you're
    asleep,
You sent men off to a distant land, your honor for
    to keep.
Fifty-eight thousand fought and died, but all were
    not brought home,
Won't you accept responsibility and help us set
    them free?

Many have died from Agent Orange, the cancer
    tells the tale,
Others suffer from Post Traumatic Stress, wonder
    why they end up in jail,
Wake up, America, you don't even know you're
    asleep,
You sent men off to a distant land, your honor for
    to keep.

In training we never heard the word defeat, we
    were willing to give all,
We fought beside men, brave and true, watched
    many a comrade fall,
You tied our hands, you lost the war, then we
    received the blame.
Don't you owe us anything? We suffered in your
    name.

Wake up, America, you don't even know you're
    asleep.
You sent men off to a distant land, your honor for
    to keep.

John Steer

CHAPTER 20

Fort Steer and Beyond

G od, I can't take it anymore."
After dealing with people in crisis — over 600 in ten years who had lived with us at Ft. Steer for anywhere from 1 week to 14 months — as my wife and I had, it takes a toll. Keeping Fort Steer in operation was a constant battle for more money, counselors, and staff. There was never enough, and the burden became overwhelming. Since we were always struggling financially, I had to be on the road a lot raising funds and preaching. The strain began to wear us down. One day as I was sitting on the back deck of my house, I prayed, "God, I can't take it anymore."

The Lord spoke to my heart, "Well, you've done what I said."

"Lord, You're not listening to me. I can't take it anymore."

It was as if the Lord spoke to my heart a second time. "You've done what I said."

"What?" I asked. "You mean I've done what You wanted me to do with Fort Steer?" The Lord just lifted the burden, and what a burden it was!

❧

Realizing that our ministry at Fort Steer would be coming to an end, I began to reflect on all we had learned. 215

One thing we discovered is that you can give somebody a place to live and clothes and food, but unless they have a reason to live, it's all in vain. That's why we changed our focus from worrying about the veteran's material needs — clothing, shelter, and money — to their spiritual condition.

Many veterans are suffering from guilt, post-traumatic stress, condemnation, or lack of self-worth. We can give people pensions and disability payments and money, but — like welfare — it won't change the circumstance of the individual. We have to find a *reason* to live versus a *place* to live. What is the only valuable and lasting reason to live?

I tell people, "The only reason worth struggling and working for the rest of your life — the only reason that will give you peace — is to accept Christ as your Saviour and to have Jesus alive in your life." That was our focus at Fort Steer — to see people's lives changed through Christ, without our becoming an organized church or overly religious. Our goal was to share our own personal experiences of how Christ changed our lives and how He can change theirs.

When Donna and I started Fort Steer in 1985, I did it because of a need — and not because I got a revelation from heaven. I saw there was a need for this kind of ministry, and I thought, *Well, we'll do this, but I need a lot of help.*

I didn't really get all the help that I felt I needed, but I depended on the Lord more and more. Eventually, I came to realize that the Scripture is true: "I can do all things through Christ who strengthens me." If you get a vision or if God speaks to your heart to do something, He'll supply you with the wherewithal to do it. He did me. I have no regrets.

~~~

"If I don't turn my life around, I'm not going to live much longer." Bill was typical of the Vietnam veterans who came to Fort Steer for help. When he arrived at Charlotte, Arkansas, however, he had a very bad attitude.

Through prayer, counseling, and Bible studies — which we had every morning — Bill accepted Jesus and his attitude completely changed. He realized that he had to make the choice to change. After being delivered from alcohol, he went back to Indiana.

A few months later I received a letter from his boss, who had previously fired him. He wrote, "Thanks a lot for getting my guy back on track. The Lord has certainly turned his life around."

As Fort Steer began to grow, we gained experience in how to minister to troubled people. I got certified as an addiction specialist and began working with the alcoholics and drug addicts who came to us. Many vets were suffering from post-traumatic disorder.

We had a lot of success stories. On one occasion I was in a supermarket in Kentucky, and a black lady came running up to me. She grabbed me and was kissing my cheek and hugging on me. I was wondering, *What in the world is going on? I don't know you, lady.*

She said, "Oh, thank you so much. You kept my husband at Fort Steer for a couple of months, and you worked with him. Now he takes us to church, and he's doing good."

It means a lot to know when our vets succeed.

Many times people I have never met will come up to me and greet me. They will thank me for praying for their husband or dad or for leading him to the Lord. Others are grateful for the support that got their loved one through the nightmares and made it possible for him to hold down a job. Such gratitude is extremely rewarding.

Over the ten years of the Fort Steer ministry, many veterans and their wives rebuilt their lives. During that time, we took in over 600 veterans — some of whom came with a wife and children. The children of parents in our program attended our little public school in Charlotte, where about 200 kids were enrolled. It was a good experience for them.

Eventually we had 14 buildings that were built with the help of various veterans groups, churches, and individuals. We paid cash for most of the building materials as they were needed, or we took out small loans and paid them off in the short term.

The judges in the area — and even from other areas —

paroled several veterans into my custody. The judge gave them a choice: "Either go to Fort Steer, get sobered up, and get your act together, or go to jail."

Avoiding jail isn't always a good motivator because some people don't really want to change; but because they have options, they take the lesser of the two punishments.

"Work is therapy," I often told the guys who came to Fort Steer. Everyone was required to work three hours a day. We generally had between 10 and 30 people on the place at a time. The guys who avoided work were the ones who never got any help. Most, however, went along with the program, whether it was sweeping the floor, doing dishes, painting, or fixing barbed wire fence.

ᴇ⏺ᴎ

I often reminded the veterans at Fort Steer, "The Scripture says if you don't work, you don't eat."

Over the years, my wife and I have dealt with over a hundred suicides of Vietnam veterans, not just at Fort Steer, but across the country. Many died from having too much time on their hands and not enough work. People who have a lot of problems need something productive to do. They don't need to sit at home with a government check, watching TV and drinking beer all day. They need to get out and be active. Some vets have only one goal in mind: To get their post-traumatic disability check. I'm not against anybody receiving a check for compensation, but when that becomes your goal in life, then you have lost your life.

It is crucial for people with problems to focus on helping somebody else. When that happens, they begin to change and become productive citizens. As Vietnam veterans, the POW/MIA issue became a focal point for us. We were concerned about the 2,300 soldiers who never returned.

I often preached the Scripture, "Give and it shall be given" (Luke 6:38).

"That's not just about money," I told the veterans at Fort Steer. "It's also about time and anything else."

218   To promote the POW/MIA issue, I suggested that the

veterans go with me to parades and wear Fort Steer t-shirts with the big cross on the back. We also carried a coffin in the parade with a POW flag over it.

Later, Ron Martin gave us a big ship on a trailer to use in the parades. On the sides of this black ship were 10,000 MIA names written in white magic marker. Family members of the missing Americans had also included messages like, "Daddy, hammer and chisel is waiting to take your name off the wall when you come home."

As we pulled the ship through the parades, I would stand in the top of it singing, "Don't Let a Wounded Soldier Die," or "God Bless the USA."

As the veterans from Fort Steer realized that hearts were being changed and that their efforts were making an impact, they began to gain more self-worth.

We worked with a lot of people, but each individual's success or failure depended on his attitude. During the first few years, Vietnam veterans came to Fort Steer with hopes of helping themselves. As time went by, more programs became available throughout the country, and vets could go other places. Some vets didn't really want to change. All they wanted was a place to live, so they went from program to program. Other veterans were more concerned about getting a post-traumatic disability pension than they were about getting their lives together. That was very disheartening.

Those who came with a positive attitude and wanted help — whether it was deliverance from alcohol or drugs or nightmares or whatever — got help. We would work with them and pray with them. We'd hug them or kick them in the butt — whatever it took to help turn their life around — as long as they wanted to help themselves.

⌖

Every year for about six years, we held a Vietnam veterans reunion at Fort Steer. Each gathering brought more and more vets and their families until we had nearly 6,000 attend the last year it was held.

Part of the attraction was the live entertainment,

including Sam the Sham, who is a good Christian brother now; Britt Small and Festival, the band I sing with occasionally; and Sammy Davis and Al Lynch, both Congressional Medal of Honor recipients.

One year we brought in "the moving wall" — a half-scale replica of the Vietnam Veteran's Memorial Wall with 58,000 names of those who died in Vietnam. School buses brought in children from as far as 40 or 50 miles away to see the wall.

During the reunion, we also presented the gospel through the preaching of the Word and testimonies from born-again veterans. My good friend, Al Riley, and his wife Linda came to all six reunions. Each year, his faith grew and grew.

After one reunion, about 10 veterans were baptized in the lake. Although Al was in a wheelchair and suffered from multiple sclerosis, he said, "I want to be baptized, too." We picked him up and carried him out in the water and baptized him. Everyone was really blessed. After that experience, Al's life changed as his love for the Lord increased.

About a year later I received a call from his Al's wife, Linda. "Al has kind of flipped out," she said, not knowing how to describe what was happening. Apparently, the MS was affecting his brain, which I guess isn't very common but does happen sometimes. "Al ran his wheelchair off the top of a flight of steps and tried to kill himself," his wife explained.

"Was he hurt?" I asked.

"No," she replied. "But a very expensive wheelchair was busted up. Now he's more frustrated than ever because he couldn't kill himself. I took him to the VA hospital psych ward to get him some help. He wasn't talking to anyone and was very angry."

"That's not the Al that I know," I said.

The disease had him confused. I was so concerned that I got a private plane to fly me to the VA hospital where he was. At first he wouldn't talk to me, he just stared out into space from his wheelchair. I finally kicked the wheelchair and said, "Hey, get your head out of your . . . butt!" — or something like that.

Then he grinned and began to talk to me. "The CIA is bugging our conversation," he told me and continued to make other paranoid expressions. I knew Al was having some serious problems. Before leaving, I prayed with him and rebuked the devil who wanted to take his life.

A few weeks later, I talked to Al and his wife. "He's out of the hospital and doing very well," Linda told me.

"Yep," Al said, "I'm getting on with my life and speaking at DAV meetings." I was thrilled to hear that he was once again helping people as he had done his whole life.

Not long after that, I received another phone call from Linda. "Al has just taken his life in the back of the van," she sobbed. "While we were driving home from a meeting, he stuck a revolver in his mouth and pulled the trigger."

Al's suicide was devastating. It crushed me. Linda asked me to give the message at the funeral, which was attended by more than 500 people. I told the crowd, "The Lord shared with me the Scripture 'to have patience with the feeble-minded.' God didn't say write them off or preach them into hell. He said have patience with them. I'm just sorry that Satan was able to destroy Al through this disease that affected his brain. And I'm sure that I'll see Al in heaven someday."

During one reunion, a little, short Jewish girl named Becky, who had been in the army and stationed in Germany, came for the first time.

John Bouldry — whom I had led to the Lord several years earlier and is now a minister of the gospel — approached her and started talking about Jesus. She said, "You ain't gonna push none of that Jesus stuff down my throat. I'm a Jew, and I don't want anything to do with it."

He said, "Okay."

He came and told me, "John, there's a gal that you've got to go talk to."

I went over and asked, "How you doing? My name's John Steer."

"My name is Becky, and you ain't pushing none of that

Jesus junk down my throat" was her curt reply.

"Hey, sweetheart, you're right. We ain't!" I replied. "I didn't come here to fight with you. I just want you to have a good time this weekend."

John Bouldry, who has a tremendous zeal for the Lord, had a burden for Becky. He started sharing with her and eventually gave her the Gospel of John. She went into a vehicle and sat there all day reading the book. Before the day was over, she was crying and telling us about her problems. Before we knew it, she had accepted Jesus as her Saviour. The next day we baptized her in the lake.

Later, Becky, who suffers from kidney failure and other diseases was in a coma for several months. As she became weaker and weaker, her husband and I began planning her funeral. Eventually, however, she regained consciousness and became stronger than ever. She remained in a lot of pain, but she realized that Jesus Christ could help her — every day.

Since the writing of this book Becky has gone on to be with Jesus.

❧

When we realized our time at Fort Steer was coming to an end, Donna and I began to interview different ministries who were interested in taking over the fort. During our ten years at Fort Steer working with veterans, we had received quite a bit of publicity and some support from various national organizations.

One day Dwayne Graham, an investigative reporter from Little Rock, came up to study the work we were doing with veterans. Later, without my knowledge, he nominated Donna and I to receive a Presidential Point of Light award, started by President George Bush.

Suddenly, people we hadn't talked to in years were calling us to say, "The awards committee contacted us about your work at Fort Steer with Vietnam veterans. They wanted us to verify certain information and confirm the success of your programs."

About a year later, Donna and I received the 682nd

Presidential Point of Light for our work with veterans. We were thrilled with the award in spite of the fact that we were waiting for another group to take over our work. It was time for us to move on to what the Lord had for us next.

Finally, a group called Christ the King Church out of Dyersburg, Tennessee, decided to use the fort to help anyone who needs help — not exclusively veterans. We feel very good about that.

My burden to help veterans come to Christ has continued to be a major focus in my life. At one time, I was national chaplain for the 173d Airborne Association. Currently, I am national chaplain for Viet Now, an organization providing support groups for Vietnam veterans and their spouses. I am also national chaplain for National Vietnam Veterans Coalition, out of Washington, D.C., which boasts over 300,000 members.

As a result of my work with veterans and my national recognition by several people and organizations, I was appointed to the Military Health Care Advisory Committee in Washington, D.C. Three or four times a year, I attend meetings with the surgeon generals of the military and the deputy secretaries of defense to provide input on our health care for our active military and retirees.

It always amuses me to think, *Here I am, with my ninth grade education, sitting down with generals, presidents, vice presidents, and dignitaries of various countries.* I can't help but smile at God's amazing way of working in the lives of His children.

Then I realize that education has nothing to do with it. God has called me and anointed me to accomplish His will in my life — and He provides the opportunities and opens the doors. Although I hope God will continue to use me to bring the gospel to veterans and their families, I also feel called to minister through music.

Over the years I've recorded nine music albums, but that was always secondary on my list of priorities. My ministry to veterans had been first. I continue to work with veterans, but now do less talking and more singing. Recently, I was awarded a recording contract with Sierra Nashville Records in Nashville, Tennessee.

I am really excited about the new direction He is moving us in our career and ministry.

You, too, are important to God. You were created, you didn't just happen; and God has a purpose for your life.

When a person accepts Christ as Saviour — whether they're a junkie or a general — he or she can begin searching for their true purpose in life. Purpose, however, means more than having a fancy home or car, or a pretty wife. Our reason for living is to allow Christ to express Himself through us. When that happens, life takes on new meaning and greater fulfillment.

Wounded soldiers don't have to die — you, too, can be healed. In Psalm 37:25 David said, "I have been young and old. But I have never seen the righteous forsaken or God's seed begging bread."

I have been to many countries and experienced many things. However, I know only one thing for sure. The bread David refers to here represents life. And the only real life we can know, the only real joy we can experience is in knowing Jesus Christ as our Saviour and having the assurance of eternal life through Him.

Jesus said:

Come unto me all ye that labour and are heavy laden and I will give you rest (Matt. 11:28).

David said:

Taste and see that the Lord is good (Ps. 34:8).